MOTHERING,
An Art of the Heart

Nine Moms with Forty-three Children
Share Their Reflections from the Empty Nest

Editors and Authors:
Suzanne Shady
Jo Ann Figueiredo

Illustrator and Author:
Patricia Costigan

Authors:
Patricia Bertucci
Diane Knittle
Mary Dahl Maher
Elizabeth O'Toole
Sheila Roney
Patricia Urban

To our mothers, who showed us the way.
To our children and grandchildren
who are the reason for it all.

Contents

"The twigs and fluff and leaves of the bird's nest are brought from all sorts of places, from wherever the brave careful mother alights, with fluttering but daring heart, to fetch them, from the distances and explorations that only the spread wings of love know. It is the shape of her breast that moulds the nest to its inviting roundness."

The Reed of God, Caryll Houselander

Mothering, an Art of the Heart

Our story has a small beginning, as most stories do. Two of us met for coffee. One began the conversation with the accomplishment of a young adult son securing a good job. During his growing years, he struggled mightily and was a cause of huge concern and many crises. The other mom acknowledged the faithfulness of her friend for her commitment to see her child through. "We should write a book!" she said.

We are nine mothers, who collectively have 43 children. Five years ago we came together for the first time and began to share our stories. With our children grown and starting lives of their own, we reflected back. We realized that the journey of motherhood taught us many lessons that were important for us to pass on. At first there was much excitement when we thought of moments when we'd taught a child something significant or learned a new parenting skill. However, the project almost floundered when we recalled how and when we'd failed. Who were we to write a book?

But we persevered. Through our storytelling, we began to identify with each other and take great comfort in the fact that we were not alone in our failures and successes. Over the next months we made slow progress. We consulted a professional project manager, also a mother, who helped us define our mission and goals. Out of our conversations eight themes emerged which we identified as important elements in raising children and building a strong family. We thought of these as the spokes of a wheel with love at its hub: joy, nurturing, socialization, values, traditions, faith, and humor.

We recognized the mother's role in guiding and developing these elements. We saw her love as central, providing the framework and unifying the whole. Love and practical experience helped us gain wisdom in the art of mothering. Wisdom, then, became the outer rim, encircling the family to maintain harmony and stability. This was no abstract philosophy, but a lived experience for each of us.

"The art of mothering is an art of the heart." When Sheila read these words as we sat together in Pat Costigan's living room, all heads nodded vigorously. We knew this to be true. Raising children called forth so much from us, whether it was learning to live together, guiding them through life challenges or building lasting relationships—we invested the best of ourselves. We fell in love with our children, never dreaming that it would require so much of us or understanding the enormity of the benefits in return.

The "mother wisdom" we received from our mothers was the huge investment of themselves, their time and attention and their commitment to family. This inspired us, consciously or not, to do the same. Through our collective sharing on wisdom, we saw that the art of mothering is a vocation of love. Not a Hallmark Card kind of love but one that faces life head on. We develop our practical skills and an understanding of raising children but the primary task is to learn to love unconditionally—hence the challenge to the very depths of our being. What a gift, not only for our children but for ourselves! Together, we've marveled at the lessons we've learned and the ways we've grown to be better persons.

The stories in this book do not represent conclusive advice on mothering but rather portray important aspects of our individual journeys. In the sharing of these experiences with other moms, we tap into a collective wisdom that is rich and powerful. While we acknowledge that there is no roadmap for raising a child, our hope is that you will benefit from our sharing these stories of mother wisdom.

Our stories were written between the joys and sorrows of family life. Within our group of nine, one mom experienced the untimely death of an adult child and was diagnosed with breast cancer; another had a son in Iraq. There were moves to new homes, renovations of old homes, launching college graduates, weddings and welcoming new grandbabies!

We are acutely aware that we have not been perfect moms nor do we have perfect children. Our families have been confronted by the many pitfalls of modern culture, often painfully so. Motherhood has been our vocation. Our varied professional careers have been our avocation. We invested ourselves in a serious and committed way to making a nest for our young. Now that they have flown off to their own lives, it's time to reflect back on the wisdom we gained through the journey. It is from a desire to share this wisdom, often hard won, that we have written this book together.

EnJoying Family Life

1

———⋘⋙———

1

Joy

EnJoying Family Life

When I was a little girl, I often spent the night at my Grammy's. One of our favorite activities was to watch *The Lawrence Welk Show*. As a child, I loved the opening of the show. Lawrence Welk would walk onstage surrounded by a magical stream of bubbles while his orchestra was playing. Grammy found joy in the opening because it was something I loved.

Like those bubbles, bursts of joy pop up in the midst of our busy lives when we least expect them. Raising children is a difficult and challenging job, and the moments of joy are times when we can recognize that our work is paying off. As adults, we need to stop to cherish these times before they fly out of reach.

Joy is the unique gift of childhood; it is naturally present in children. As we grow older, our ability to find joy in small things fades. Through our children, we can once again find the simple joys in life. Our desire as mothers is to create an atmosphere in which joy can flourish.

One dictionary defines joy as "the emotion of great happiness," but joy is so much more than an emotion. It's an important facet of family life. It's the fruit of love and is captured in the relationship between a parent and child. As mothers, each of us has found joy to be an experience that sometimes has caught us unaware.

This chapter on joy is not meant to provide a yardstick by which to try to measure all experience. Instead it is a wee bit of advice to all of us to be open to the evanescence of the unexpected in our daily lives.

Elizabeth O'Toole

Guitar Hero

It quickly became the standard bath time ritual. Two, three, or four wriggly grubby bodies jumped into the bubbly water with favorite toys and the requisite floating soap and were transformed into the most loyal groupies ever. Daddy was the headliner every evening with his 12-string guitar and the songs were familiar fare: the Beatles, Elvis and selections from *Wee Sing Silly Songs*. How it originally came about we might never remember but it was so much fun that it was repeated night after night for years—or so it seems.

Yes, it was bath time, but it was also family time. Little did the waterlogged fans realize that Dad was there to supervise practice in good grooming. For sure, they never knew Mom was putting the youngest to bed and bustling through the adjacent bedrooms, collecting dirty clothes and getting ready for drying and pajama detail.

Ah, memories! When daughter number 2 got married she chose an interesting song to dance to with her dad. "When I'm 64" rang through the hall and brought to our minds a small bathroom and damp towels and a rousing chorus of young voices sharing in the fun.

Jo Ann Figueiredo

Moments of Mother Bliss

- Bath time was play time for our two-year-old daughter... The water dripped from the faucet into her bath water. The droplets popped back up to the surface. She screeched in delight, "Look, Mommy, water puppets!"

- Getting up for school was not always easy for our first grader. One windy March morning she lagged in bed. In exasperation I called from the kitchen, "What are you doing in there?" "Laying in bed looking out the window watching the trees say 'yes' and 'no'."

- Three-year-old Peter and two-year-old Mary were snuggled in bed with me. Peter got up and put on his plastic fireman's hat, raincoat and boots. He took the vacuum cleaner hose and pretended to spray the room. When he tired of his game he took off his fire-fighting gear and crawled back into bed. Mary, sucking her thumb, took it out long enough to whisper to him, "Fireman, you boo-ti-ful."

- Beth was a very little girl with a big imagination. She went to an imaginary school she called "Gratherskeets," named after its principal. She had friends there named, "George O." and "Black." George O. had a red sports car. One day she came stamping in from the sandbox with a very annoyed look on her face. I said, "Honey, what is the matter?" Her reply, "Mr. Gratherskeets said I had to take a nap." And into her bed she went!!

Diane Knittle

Homemade Joy

My daughter Caitlin had just turned four and was excited that Christmas was fast approaching. We visited the library and among her selection of books was *Merry Christmas, Ernest and Celestine,* by Gabrielle Vincent. It was the story of two good friends, a bear and a mouse. They had no money but worked very hard to be creative with what they had in order to host a party for their friends. They were filled with joy when they were able to celebrate Christmas with their friends, giving much of themselves.

Caitlin loved this story. We read it several times and she was inspired to make gifts for everyone who was joining us that Christmas. Like the characters in the story, her gifts would hang on the Christmas tree waiting for their recipients. She enlisted my help to gather materials—paper, crayons, rickrack, and ribbon. Her plan was to make pictures for everyone using Christmas-related themes. Her joy was boundless as she drew the Holy Family in a manger for one gift, the sheep and cows for another, the Wise Men, Christmas tree, wreath, candles, snowman, holly—anything to do with Christmas. Each one needed to be original. With care, the completed pictures were rolled, ribboned, and hung on our tree.

On Christmas day, Caitlin's joy was contagious as she handed each relative their gift. In turn, the pictures were unrolled, examined, and shared. Caitlin, the youngest member of our extended family, was engaged in conversation and complimented by grandparents, aunts and uncles. These drawings, prepared with love and care, enhanced our family's delight in celebrating Christmas together.

Sheila Roney

If you were all alone in the universe
With no one to talk to,
no one with which to share the beauty of the stars,
to laugh with, to touch, what would be your purpose
in life?
It is other life; it is love, which gives your life meaning.
This is harmony.
We must discover the joy of each other,
the joy of challenge, the joy of growth.

—Mitsugi Saotome

Take Two

One rainy early spring day, my two older children were playing together in the house. It was late afternoon and I was thinking of what to prepare for dinner. It may have been the weather and being cooped up in the house, but I was not feeling especially energetic or cheerful. My daughter and son, on the other hand, had plenty of energy.

"Mom," my almost-four-year-old son said as he came wheeling into the kitchen on his riding toy. "We're playing that we're going to Aunt Jean's. You be Aunt Jean and be surprised when we get here, OK?" My husband's youngest sister, Jean, lived several hours away from us and our children loved having her visit. She was a lot of fun and had boundless energy to play with them and listen to their stories. I must admit the last thing I felt like doing was playing pretend but I agreed. The two of them snuck down the stairs to the side door and knocked.

"Who is it?" I asked half-heartedly. They came bursting up the stairs and yelled, "Hi, Aunt Jean! Surprise! It's us!" Without much zeal I responded, "Oh, hi, Bridget and Brian. How did you get here?" The looks on their faces said it all. I had failed. Brian was the one who spoke: "Mom, that's not how Aunt Jean would be!!! She'd be excited and happy to see us!"

I knew exactly what he meant. I did not give of myself to these two wonderful children who were enjoying a game of pretend. Chastened, I admitted my lack of enthusiasm and asked if we could do it again. It took only a few moments of my time and a tiny bit of energy to feign surprise, excitement, enthusiasm.

I have drawn on this memory over the years to remind me that sometimes it takes a little bit of extra effort to make an ordinary day more enjoyable for those you love. But it is worth it.

Sheila Roney

"If you want to put more joy in your life, put more effort into the things you do. We get more satisfaction and joy from things we have worked hard on, than we do from things that come easily to us."
—Edward W. Smith, *Sixty Seconds to Success*

Joyful Rewards

For many years I longed to be a mother. That longing was finally realized with the gift of a precious baby girl through adoption. What unspeakable joy! Soon, however, I learned that desire is one thing and reality quite another.

One cool autumn morning when Anna Mary was about 2 ½, we came downstairs for an early breakfast. She was wearing a little peach nightie that I had made for her, one of my first and rare sewing projects. After spending time together at the breakfast table chatting about many topics, we moved to the living room floor. I brought Anna some toys and spread out the newspaper, hoping to catch a few minutes of relaxation before beginning the day. Anna was content for a little while but was soon peppering me with questions, "When are we going to the park? Are we going in the car? Why are the leaves red?" and on and on. Diversion with picture books lasted an even briefer while. Then, determined to get my attention, she happily closed in for a hug, content to rock on my back in seesaw fashion.

I was completely exasperated and annoyed. Couldn't I have even ONE adult moment to read the newspaper? It seemed like there was never any time for myself. I was impatient and lost my temper too often. Mothering was way harder than I bargained for.

Then I remembered a happier moment. We were settled in to read a bedtime story, *A Pocket for Corduroy* by Don Freeman, one of Anna's favorites. As I began reading she would finish the sentences on each page, with complete accuracy and perfect intonation. She had memorized the text. This tiny little girl with an even tinier cherubic voice read *me* the bedtime story. I was dazzled.

I praised Anna's accomplishment while she giggled and reveled in the attention. What a joyful moment! Soon Dad and grandparents got to share in this treat.

Such moments of joy saved me. Days with a two-year-old left me exhausted and depleted. But moments that were milestones, or a warm hug and wet kiss, or her spontaneous delight with life, all drew me closer to her, helping me see that I was making a difference in her life and encouraging me to stay the course.

Suzanne Shady

Vacation Time

Many of the most joyful times in our family's life came during family outings. I loved watching our young children's windswept faces while riding in a motorboat, seeing 6-year-old Ray catch pan-fish from the dock at dusk and sharing Anna's excitement at 13 when she mastered water skiing with those long skinny legs that seemed to be two thirds of her total height. Whether it was climbing Little Bear Mountain with all the cousins in the Adirondacks or making the best of a week of rainy days at the ocean, there was a pleasure in sharing it as a family.

Best of all was just hanging out, like we did last August, sitting around the campfire, watching the panorama of the stars coming out over the lake. It held us entranced late into the night as we chatted and pointed out satellites, constellations, and a shooting star. Now we were with our grown children, daughter-in-law and boyfriend, aunts and uncles, nieces and nephews all savoring a moment of joy.

Suzanne Shady

"How necessary it is to cultivate a spirit of joy."
—Dorothy Day

Beach Joy

My feet hit the grainy, cold sand and sometimes the salty surf as I briskly hiked along Nauset Beach. The sun peeked around and through wispy white clouds that dotted the sky. Would I see a seal on this jaunt? Would I see other walkers along that stretch of the beach? I picked up my pace as I attempted to warm my body after riding the waves in the 62° water. My body warmed and so did my soul. I felt a surge of electrifying joy, of closeness to God, of thankfulness for my family, of gratitude for alone time to reflect on all the blessings in my life. I was excited to turn around and return to my family. I was refreshed, revitalized, joyful and ready to pass on that exuberance.

As I approached my children and husband on their blankets spread on the sand, I thought of how they always teased me when I said, "Nauset Beach is Cape Cod to me." After thirty years of family vacations on Cape Cod, I knew they understood the fun of breakfast on the beach after stopping to buy donuts on the way. I knew they appreciated the cold but exhilarating time in the water. I knew they also pondered the beauty of the beach, sand dunes, and majestic waves. However, I'm not sure I'd ever expressed to them the joy of walking the beach alone, and basking in God's nature with the realization that I was a very blessed woman. This was the day to do it.

Patricia Bertucci

"Joy is the serious business of heaven."

—C.S.Lewis

Joy Happens

Joy happened all around and within our family when my children were little and throughout their teen years. It happened, but I was separated from it for many years, caught in the darkness of depression. I did not feel the joy, but the important part of this story is that joy happened in spite of what was going on inside my head. Joy happened. It percolated from within the children; it was inherent in them.

Joy is like the wind. We cannot see the wind, but we can see the effects of wind blowing on the trees. Most of the time I could not feel the joy, but I could see joy in those extraordinary moments as it rippled through my husband, Bob, and through our girls in their smiles, giggles, laughter, and awe.

Life within a family can be difficult, even painful. I did find that it was little joys breaking through spontaneously at times that gave me relief and a feeling of light-heartedness.

Patricia Costigan

Hannah's Song

I've got the joy, joy, joy, joy down in my heart.
Where? Down in my heart!
Where? Down in my heart!
I've got the joy, joy, joy, joy down in my heart,
down in my heart
down in my heart to stay.
—George Willis Cooke

Joy is an elusive feeling to grab hold of and describe. I recall ebullient, playful moments: the joy in the smiles generated by my young children as they successfully kept a multicolored kite up in the sky, discovered the subtle beauty of seashells collected along the beach, or screamed with delight at the gentle falling of winter's first snowflakes. At the same time I also think of a deeper meaning that I associate with a line from scripture in which Luke writes that "Mary kept all these things and pondered them in her heart." This reminds me that joy is also like a faithful friend who is there to nurture and guide even when the moments are not so playful.

Whenever I hear the word joy, I think of my chubby-cheeked, blue-eyed, three-year-old daughter Hannah, our fourth child and first girl. She was born five days after my husband and I made a cross country car trip from El Paso, Texas, to northern Virginia with her three brothers, aged four to nine. Our little Mazda station wagon was crammed with all the possessions we could fit into it along with an emergency delivery pack given to me by my former colleagues in the Labor and Delivery Unit. She was exactly five days overdue when she arrived.

We were making the kind of exodus that many face in times of economic crisis. My husband was one of the last teachers at a well-established language institute before it completely closed. We couldn't pay our bills on my income as a registered nurse, especially since I was going to be on maternity leave. When my husband was offered a position to start immediately in suburban Washington, D.C., we struggled with the decision as to whether I should stay in El Paso and move after the baby was born or if we should all go together. My heart ached as I thought of my husband missing the birth and I couldn't begin to fathom packing and selling a house with a newborn, three active little boys and a mother from New York, just diagnosed with a possible return of colon cancer during her short stay with us. So we opted for the family trip together and I was actually doing our first grocery shopping when I went into labor, for once happy that the baby was coming late. There was certainly joy in the relief of the safe journey to Reston, Virginia, and in finding a place to live before Hannah's birth and there was joy in her arrival coinciding with the news that my mother didn't have another tumor.

But the joy that I reflexively recall is the animated face of my little girl, a few years later, as she would sing and enthusiastically act out the words to the children's song called, "I've Got the Joy." This was not simply a mother's delight in her daughter; my joy came from the memory of all that had brought us to that moment.

Mary Dahl Maher

A Prescription for Stay-At-Home Fever

The three years following Hannah's birth were very difficult. Our daily lives changed dramatically as we moved from a comfortable and spacious ranch home nestled into the side of the Sandia Mountain Range to a cramped condominium in the very fast-paced, upwardly mobile, and expensive suburban lifestyle of the nation's capital. As much as I desired to be a stay-at-home mom, I knew no one in a town where it seemed all women worked during the day. There was no one to talk to but my children.

In desperation, I approached the pastor of our new parish. He told me of another woman who was experiencing a similar sense of isolation and who had just asked to put a notice in the church bulletin about starting a mothers' group. The first week, there were twelve women. By the third meeting we had grown to over fifty and divided into different interest areas. More importantly, we had turned the sorrow of feeling alone into a joy multiplied not only among the 50 of us, but our small children and husbands as well. Little did we realize the joy we would find when, out of loneliness, we sought the company of other mothers.

Mary Dahl Maher

Contagious Joy

My shy and timid daughter had just entered a local Catholic school for girls. In the fall of her freshman year, Colleen had the opportunity to partake in a "Strides against Breast Cancer Walk" at a baseball park located in our city's urban core. As a part of the curriculum at her new school, participation in the walk was provided as an opportunity to earn extra physical education credit. Colleen was very excited to attend and was planning to meet some of her new friends at the walk.

I, however, was apprehensive. I was unsure about how many thousands of people would be there, and I was leaving my child "alone" in the city. What kind of a mother was I? I should have been walking with her, but I had other responsibilities that day. I knew she had to attend. I had to let go to let her grow.

I reluctantly dropped her off at the gate with her friends. She assured me she would be fine. I promised to return when it was over.

When I returned a few hours later, I was concerned as to what I would say if she'd not had a wonderful time. However, my worries were alleviated as I saw Colleen, walking out of the gate, grinning from ear to ear. She was happily chatting with her friends and totally unaware of my presence. Once she realized I was there, she bounded towards me with arms wide open and flung herself into my arms, nearly knocking me over. "Oh Mommy, Mommy, we had such fun! I'm glad I came, thank you so much for letting me! You'll have to come next year, I absolutely loved it!" My concerns dissolved. Her joy was simply contagious.

Elizabeth O'Toole

"Life isn't a matter of milestones, but moments."
—*Rose Kennedy*

Lost and Found

Noel, age 13, was missing! We called and yelled—no Noel. We were at a state park on a peninsula that had a great beach and an island not very far out on the lake. Since all of the children were good swimmers for their ages, we didn't realize that he was missing at first. He had told one of his siblings that he was going to swim out to the island. Suddenly a storm had come up with very high waves and we had called everyone in. But Noel was nowhere to be seen.

My husband decided to swim out to the island, but before he got half way, he realized that he couldn't make it and returned. We called and waved arms, but no Noel. The wind and the waves had gotten too strong for anyone to swim. We were getting panicky. This was before cell phones so we decided I would take the car with the three youngest children to find a park attendant.

As we were changing our clothes and putting wet things into bags in the car, our oldest son, Steve, shouted, "There's Noel! He's walking along the shore of the mainland." We all ran along the shore and nearly knocked him over with hugs. "Are you all right?" "What happened?" "How come you're walking?" "We last saw you swimming." When we all stopped talking Noel said, "It was farther than I had thought and the wind had picked up coming from the shore. I knew that I couldn't swim back so I walked around the island and found a calm bay between the island and the mainland on the other side. I swam over and started walking on the shore to meet you. I know you should always swim with a buddy." We had a huge hug celebration. Then we changed into dry clothes and rejoiced to be crowded altogether in the car once again. There was a refreshment stand down the road a few miles and that day we decided that the hot chocolate there was "The Best."

Patricia Urban

Universal Connection

When my son, a soldier, was on his first tour of duty in Iraq, I couldn't speak with him often and didn't know where he was. That was really hard, not knowing. Even when we spoke, I learned little due to the restrained nature of the calls. The miles of separation took their toll and I felt disconnected from him. One day, an early morning phone call awoke me from my sleep. I knew it was Tom. As we were talking, he told me, "Mom, the land is so vast. It's so barren out here. I can see millions of stars. Look out the window. We're looking at the same stars, aren't we?"

In that single unexpected moment, my worries melted and I felt a deep pride that Tom was my son. The miles faded. I knew he was safe and that we would always be connected, no matter the circumstances.

Elizabeth O'Toole

"A mother laughs our laughs, sheds our tears, returns our love, fears our fears. She lives our joys, cares our cares, and all our hopes and dreams, she shares."
—Julia Summers

When I Get to Heaven I Want to Be Six

"When I get to heaven I want to be six," read the unexpected, late night Instant Message (IM) from my son, a midshipman at the Naval Academy. Apparently the pressures of studies and military duties were overwhelming him at the end of a very long day.

"What was special about being six?" I wrote. The IMs continued:

Pjknitt: Oh, the trips to the apple farm. Riding the hay wagon out to pick apples.

Navymomma: What about walking the Bird Song trail at the park? The chickadees landed on your outstretched hand to take the seed.

Pjknitt: I loved my first Little League game playing catcher. The family in the stands cheering me on!

Navymomma: Lake Bonaparte! What great times… waterskiing…campfires…s'mores.

And so it went for another fifteen minutes. The joy of these memories not only relieved the stress my son was feeling but connected us to wonderful times of togetherness and new joy in being together again.

Diane Knittle

Nurturing

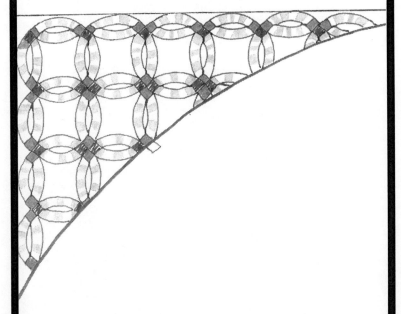

Love and Attention
for Healthy Growth

2

"Loving a child is a circular business...the more you give, the more you get, the more you get, the more you want to give."
—Penelope Leach

2

Nurturing

Love and Attention for Healthy Growth

Piece by piece a quilt is made. Scraps of fabric are stitched together to make a blanket of beauty, a blanket of warmth, a blanket of love to spread more beauty, warmth and love. Mothers are like quilts. Piece by piece a mother's life is formed and sewn together with experiences from childhood to motherhood. Piece by piece a mother is nurtured, so she can blanket her child with the same love and attention.

Today science is showing that a mother's nurturing has a tremendous impact on a child's development.

In Shelly E. Taylor's book, *The Tending Instinct: How Nurturing is Essential to Who We Are and How We Live*, she states, "We are people who tend to one another's needs, especially during stressful times. And through these actions, we have the capacity to shape one another's biology and temperament to a degree previously unimagined."

This can be a frightening thought. However, it need not be, for Shelly Taylor also says that instinct and the nurturing experiences we have received help us be available to our children.

When our oldest daughter Sarah became pregnant, she was very concerned about her ability to be a parent. She asked for advice from friends and relatives, mothers and daughters. One piece of advice she received over and over was to find another new mother to walk with her through her experiences as a mom. This bond between mothers nurtures, strengthens, supports.

On July 13, 2008, Sarah gave birth to our first grandchild, Mica. A mere 16 hours later my husband, daughter Erica, and I were there to make Mica's first week in this world a week to celebrate a new baby, a new mother and a new father. We were all intent on caring for and protecting this new person. We were there to nurture her and to tend to her mother as well. We walked with Mica, bathed her, read and sang to her, made meals, did laundry and created a special world for Mica and her parents to begin their life together. Sarah and Mica basically lived that first week in an insulated cocoon, safe and protected.

Then it was time to put Mica in her car seat for her first trip to the doctor. Sarah expressed how hard it was to take Mica out and make her vulnerable to the outside world. However, Sarah also said that she, her husband, Jason, family and friends would protect and care for Mica until she could handle the world on her own.

As mothers we nurture to promote healthy growth. That seems like an overwhelming task! However, we need to remember that just as women have gotten together to make quilts and also to repair them, mothers have also nurtured and been nurtured. As the nine of us reminisced on this topic, we realized that it was difficult to remember those basic things that colored the everydayness of our lives, the mundane tasks we took for granted as we moved through our families' growing up years. So we talked to rekindle our memories and we began to discern a pattern of gifts handed from mother to daughter, friend to friend, mom to mom and daughter back to mother and that is where we found our stories.

The stories in this chapter highlight the fact that nurturing is more than just repetitive motions that satisfy basic needs. These chores are suffused with care, thought, and love. The children involved respond with their own unbounded love, which encourages us as moms to persevere. Nurturing becomes a dynamic process of giving and receiving that impacts all those involved. This giving and receiving, and the close relationships such care and attention creates, sustained all of us, parent and child alike, through the trials of guiding our children through their childhoods and teens and into adulthood.

Our stories also reflect a new shift in our lives and now we find that our adult children are nurturing us, cooking meals that nourish body and soul, managing family gatherings, and sometimes hosting us in their homes. With some poignancy we also recognize that we have come full circle as we nurture our parents through aging, sickness and their dying days. As mothers we have worked to keep these circles of nurturing love and attention going strong, enriching the growth of our children and ultimately strengthening our families, neighborhoods and communities.

Patricia Bertucci

Who Ever Heard of a "Beancot?"

Beth had a mind of her own at a very early age. Even as a baby, there were foods she would try and others she wouldn't. Her all time favorite was apricots. Try as we might to introduce new foods, she would resist. One day, when attempting to give her applesauce, I tried a new approach.

"Here is some applecot," I told her. She took it and ate it right up. So, I tried a different one..."beancot"... and she ate it! We were able to get a variety of foods into her if she thought they were related to her favorite, apricots. One morning shortly thereafter I heard her singing in her crib, "mommy-cot," "daddy-cot," and "bottle-cot." From then on she added "cot" to anything that appealed to her. Follow your instincts. It pays to be creative.

Diane Knittle

"Your family and your love must be cultivated like a garden. Time, effort, and imagination must be summoned constantly to keep any relationship flourishing and growing."

—Jim Rohn

Playpen Haven

My mother made sure all her daughters had a Pack 'n Play a.k.a. playpen when we started our families. We weren't necessarily sold on the concept of penning up our children—after all, we came of age in the '70s—but we went along and it soon became one of the most valuable pieces of equipment I ever owned.

With the first couple of babies it was my drop zone. If a bathroom break was necessary or the laundry needed tending in the basement or the phone rang or the stove was hot, I knew the safest place for the baby was the playpen.

As our family grew, this humble spot took on another job of equal importance for the younger members of the family. It was the place where they were safe from the man-handling that they got from the older kids. When Emily was born, her older siblings were four, three, and two years old and they *loved* their new baby. It was dangerous to leave her anywhere where they could get their hands on her. They hugged and kissed her with such abandon that it would reduce her to tears. Her life was much less stressful when she was inside looking out, beyond the reach of all that loving. The older siblings also had to be taught that throwing toys at her was not helpful. But she did thrive being safe, still in close proximity to the rest of the family's hustle and bustle.

Jo Ann Figueiredo

One-on-One Time

When Steve was three, Dave was two, and Michelle was 6 months old, most afternoons I needed a nap more than they did. I would sit in the big chair with all of them on my lap after lunch and read a story with lots of pictures and interruptions. Then Michelle was tucked into the crib, and the two boys went into their room and climbed into their beds. I would let them choose a record. We had quite a number of them with stories that lasted between 30 or 40 minutes and that afforded me a little recoup time! When the record was over they could get up *quietly* and come downstairs. Often they would fall asleep before it was finished. If one woke up before the other it was always special time with Mom for that child. We would put together a puzzle, bake cookies, and play until the others woke up.

Patricia Urban

Bridget's Gift

It was a beautiful summer day as my husband, our three children and I walked up the street to our neighbors' house, just two doors away. Bridget, our oldest child, had been invited to join our neighbors and their daughter, who was Bridget's best friend, on a week's vacation to Lake George.

We were there to wave good-bye and wish them a safe trip. Amid the farewell hugs and kisses, Bridget told her brother and sister that she would bring them something from her trip.

Mid-week we received a post-card from Bridget saying she was having a wonderful time. One of the vacation days was spent in town; they had gone shopping and she and her friend bought matching T-shirts and bracelets, the highlight of the trip for these ten-year-old girls. She also wrote that, as a result of spending her money on these things, she would not be able to bring the kids anything. While Brian at age 8 took this in stride, Caitlin was distressed to tears when she heard. She mentioned again the next day how disappointed she was.

And then on Saturday morning, the day of Bridget's return, Caitlin said to me, "Bridget *is* going to bring me something...L-O-V-E...and lots of it—and that's a gift!" Needless to say, tears filled my eyes at how my little darling could understand something so profound at five years of age.

Sheila Roney

A Little Night Music

Thank goodness the girls don't remember this incident because it does not reflect well on their parents. My husband and I on the other hand remember it vividly. At the time we only had our first two darling little girls. Darling One was 15 months older and she had been a handful as an infant.

She seemed to have been born restless; never a good sleeper she gave up her nap before she turned one and always struggled to settle down at night. So we were "trained" by this imp to react slowly to fussing at night; there never seemed to be a reason why she was up, except, that she wanted to be. Now Darling Two was a great sleeper; she never made a peep and snuggled right down every time, day or night. That is until she was about 6 months old. It was after midnight and we were all asleep when daddy and I awoke to some loud, dare I say demanding, crying coming from the girls' room. We lay there in bed horrified to be reliving the nightmare of those long dark nights with the first baby. We knew it was the younger one but decided to let her cry it out as we had the older one and eventually (it seemed like hours before she stopped) we all fell back to sleep.

When morning came I was quite refreshed by my night's sleep and hurried to check on the girls. There in her crib was poor Darling Two. She had thrown up hours before and was lying asleep in her mess! What a mess it was too! It had dripped onto the floor, and was all over the crib, in every nook and cranny. Her hair, stuck up straight and her pajamas once soaked were encrusted with the dried mess! It was a very sad moment for the two adults who had failed abysmally at their job of tender loving care! We learned a valuable lesson that day. Darling One and Darling Two and all subsequent Darlings would have to be taken at their word. We could not assume that the actions of one were in any way indicative of what any other child might do or require.

Ironically, Darling One who was sleeping in her big girl bed right next to the crib and who could have come to get us had never woken up.

Jo Ann Figueiredo

Hiking (Dis) Comfort

When asked about nurturing times in her child-hood, my oldest daughter, Clare, reminded me of the happiness she experienced being outdoors. Activities like hiking, camping, sledding, skiing, and running, gave her a feeling of comfort. She had a sense of being hugged by the trees and by Mother Earth.

I was very surprised because when she was about ten, our family joined a hiking club. Our girls seemed to dis-like it intensely, but Clare now describes it as a love/hate experience. As the oldest, she liked to be the leader of each hike and when we walked as a family, she always was. But in a relatively large group of experienced hik-ers, this never happened. Not being first was her frus-tration with the club. But she loved being in nature, which gave her a sense of freedom. Clare felt Mother Earth comforting and nurturing her inner self. She felt as if things were right and drew strength from it.

Clare's remarks surprised me because our four girls continually fought when we gathered for the Saturday hikes. I remember being embarrassed by my children's testy behavior when other kids seemed so agreeable. I was reminded that as with many family experiences, starting an activity may be difficult, but ultimately it may reap a positive outcome, even a lifetime of enriching results.

Patricia Costigan

When You Thought I Wasn't Looking

When you thought I wasn't looking, I saw you
hang up my first painting on the refrigerator,
and I wanted to paint another one.
When you thought I wasn't looking, I saw
you feed a stray cat,
and I thought it was good to be kind to animals.
When you thought I wasn't looking,
I saw you make my favorite cake for me
and I knew that little things are special things.
When you thought I wasn't looking,
I heard you say a prayer,
and I believed there is a God I could always talk to.
When you thought I wasn't looking,
I felt you kiss me good night, and I felt loved.
When you thought I wasn't looking, I saw that you cared,
and I wanted to be everything that I could be.
When you thought I wasn't looking, I LOOKED...
and wanted to say thanks for all the things I saw
when you thought I wasn't looking.

—Connie Back

The Mother of all Road Trips

It was a warm day in June when Irene, our almost three-year-old, came bouncing down the stairs proudly announcing: "I'm potty trained!" My husband responded, "No you're not!" The next week, our family was taking off for Alaska from Rochester, New York, by car. So, we began the trip with Irene wearing diapers in her car seat. Anne, age five, Beth, age six, and Clare, age eight, were belted in. Debbie Dog was free to roam what was left of the minivan's space.

We took a number of camping trips when our daughters were young but the most memorable and longest of our travels was to Anchorage, Alaska. The first hour of each trip was "the bird hour." Our children were like little birds in their nest at evening time, chirping to each other, "Move over, this is my space, that's my book, she looked at me funny, (cry) ... she is out of her seat belt."

We bonded well that summer. It came in many forms: game time, singing time, tourist time, eating time, seatbelt check time, and as painful as it was, time addressing unresolved issues like the arguing and competition of sibling rivalry that plagued our daily lives back home. Bob called them "team building and '70s sensitivity sessions all wrapped up into one." In our small car space, no one could flee into another room to get away from the problem; it had to be addressed. Once all six of us crammed into a restaurant booth made for four and the server asked if we would like another chair or a bigger table. Everyone was surprised. We were squished cheekby-jowl in that booth but it felt normal considering the past several weeks in the minivan. Finally in unison, we responded, "No thank you, we are quite comfortable."

While traveling twelve thousand miles in 18 days, our family learned to nurture each other. There were no TVs, movies, or external distractions. It was not always idyllic; actually, it was quite tense at times, but we evolved. When we stopped in Edmonton, Canada, for a half way break and a rare hotel stay, three-year-old Irene lamented, "I want to go home." "Where's that?" we asked her. After a short pause, she said, "In the car." The strengthened relationships in the van had comforted Irene.

After that ambitious summer, the girls learned to rely more on each other for nurturing, support, and entertainment. Car trips never again seemed daunting.

Patricia Costigan

Fine Art

Nurturing your child as she grows may not always be as straightforward or obvious as when she was a baby. When Bridget was an infant, nurturing was loving, feeding, holding, rocking, changing diapers, talking, and soothing her cries. As she grew, I offered new experiences and support to help her walk, talk, identify people and objects, and express her desires in an acceptable manner. When she ventured into the larger world at school, I held her hand as she walked into that new environment. While I wasn't perfect at it, I felt that I was helping my daughter face the challenges of her world.

In elementary school, instrument instruction was offered along with being part of the band or orchestra. Bridget chose the flute. I loved the band performances and hoped she would join the music group that played during Mass at her high school. However, during the spring of her freshman year as she was filling out her schedule for sophomore year, she said she wanted to take the art class. Unfortunately, she could not take both art and music, and her father and I needed to approve her schedule.

I knew she liked to draw but was not aware that art was something she wanted to pursue. What I did know was that she had invested a lot of time and effort in playing in the school band. I wanted her to do both, but that was not a choice. We talked about the six years she had spent learning and playing, but Bridget was resolute that she wanted to take the art class. We consented.

Not only did she take the class at school, but asked for lessons at the Memorial Art Gallery as her Christmas present that year. She registered for the class and instead of holding her hand as she walked into the classroom, I provided the transportation to get her there. Over the next two years, she attended some classes from their Saturday offerings as well as continuing her art class at school.

Bridget's reward came junior year. There was going to be a Teacher/Student exhibit and her teacher had chosen Bridget to exhibit with her. We were all so excited. The piece was a still life done with color pencils. What a thrill when our family went to the exhibit and saw Bridget's work hanging there.

Her senior year, Bridget had an entry in the regional Scholastic Art Show which is reviewed by a panel of judges. It was a metal and paper sculpture, and she was awarded a Silver Key. Obviously, she was an artist.

On one of her college applications, Bridget incorporated her drawings into the required essay and won a scholarship. She continued her study of art in college and thrived on the challenges of the assigned projects. When she had to declare a major, Bridget found herself in a dilemma. Her heart was with her art, but she also was trying to be practical about the future. After several conversations, I told her to follow her heart. How proud and thrilled we were once again when we saw her work displayed in the Senior Art Show.

As I thought back to her time with the flute and band, I never saw this passion or drive. I had listened to her and learned what she needed to be happy just as

I had had to learn when she was a baby. By listening, I trusted her, followed her lead and this allowed her talent to flourish. While her livelihood comes not from her artwork, she finds contentment in using her artistic abilities for personal enjoyment. And many of her family and friends have enjoyed the benefit of her talent as well.

Sheila Roney

"One of the important things to learn about parenting is that the more you worry about a child the less the child will worry about him or herself... instead of worrying, watch with fascination and wonder as your child's life unfolds, and help the child take responsibility for his or her own life."

—Charlotte Davis Kasl

Puppy Power

I wasn't a big fan of pets. Dogs, cats, fish, gerbils…I never grew up with them. But as my family grew, we've been through the whole menagerie…even mice, a turtle and a guinea pig. I now see the value of pets for children. The most beloved of all our pets was our dog, Belle.

Growing through puberty can be a greater challenge for some children than others. Our son struggled with identity and adoption issues in his early teen years. He wasn't open to hugs or comfort from his dad or me. The power of touch came from Belle who helped nurture him on the way to wholeness. Lying on the floor with an arm around Belle or playing tug-of-war with her gave him the unconditional love he needed. She gave him the ability to cope with his emotional challenges and accept the touch of friends and family during his teen years and beyond.

Diane Knittle

Thank You, Mrs. Spielberg

*"One thing I learned indirectly from Leah is that
you always encouraged me in everything I did.
I think that gave me a confidence in myself."*

—Suzanne's son, Ray, 26 years old, married to Leah.

Looking back on my early parenting days, I saw what restrictive parents we were and wondered if we should have lightened up—we allowed no toy guns, no Barbie Dolls, no video games or TV on school nights, etc. So when I asked my son for his thoughts and he responded with the above, I was taken aback. "Oh, you mean like the way we encouraged you with your inventions?" I inquired. "Yes definitely," he replied, "but it was for everything I was involved in." Truth be told, we tried to encourage him in lots of directions: basketball camp, another year of flute, Cub Scouts, which he flatly refused to pursue. But when he became passionate about making a skateboard, taking apart an old household appliance or pole-vaulting, we followed his lead. In high school a friend even lured him into Boy Scouts, where strong leaders nurtured his spirit of adventure and creativity. Yes, timing is all.

With Ray's comment, I started to recall those inventions of his. When he was a sixth grader, he wanted to make a "water balloon launcher" for the neighborhood picnic. I suggested he ride his bike into the village and ask the man in the upholstery shop if he had any large furniture springs he could spare. So he did. Then Ray found a PVC pipe section in our basement, cut out a wooden circle with a handle, inserted it into the pipe and created a very powerful "weapon of mass destruction" (WMD). Fortunately, the balloon was blown to smithereens upon impact, so the WMD never appeared in public.

Over the years, I did encourage Ray in those pursuits, for example, taking him to the vacuum repair shop to beg for an old appliance so he could create a "hover-craft" vehicle that would float on a cushion of air. No luck, but he had great fun taking apart every bolt and belt of a vacuum cleaner. In seventh grade after he made a set of armor out of aluminum sheeting, I introduced him to Al, a man who made replica medieval armor. Soon Ray was making chain mail, first out of old coat hangers and then for Al as an apprentice. This became a passionate hobby that appealed to his romantic sensibilities learning about great knights of old, while getting down and dirty hammering iron and cold-forging swords.

Ray's creative endeavors got increasingly bolder and more daring: a potato gun, a street luge made out of two skate boards attached under a big board, a car bought at the police auction and taken apart in our driveway. My angst over vacuuming up scraps of chain mail soon switched to worrying about life and limb.

I remember reading once that Steven Spielberg's mother used to help him blow up all kinds of things in their back yard while he was growing up. That knowledge gave me satisfaction when a young Ray and I were conspiring together on projects, and then later no small measure of hope when he took off on his own as a teen and young adult. He concluded our discussion by saying, "You know where we took the street luge, don't you? We rode it down Turk Hill Road at midnight!"

Perhaps not surprisingly, Ray went on to become a mechanical engineer and works for a medical device company creating new and better pacemakers and defibrillators. He still takes apart engines, rebuilds antique cars and creates new inventions.

As a parent you try to find activities that suit your child's temperament or interests, knowing they can't try everything, and yet recognizing the mystery of this evolving human being. I discovered there are times when you are filled with awe and delight and other times fright and alarm, wondering who this child will become. Nurturing is the process of creating an environment in which your child can blossom. The adventure is in discovering whether the bloom will be as exotic as a bird of paradise, as bold as a sunflower or something entirely new.

Suzanne Shady

"If a child is to keep his inborn sense of wonder, he needs the companionship of at least one adult who can share it, rediscovering with him the joy, excitement and mystery of the world we live in."

—Rachel Carson

Timothy Comes Home

The smell of a newborn, the warm nuzzle of his head under your chin, as you inhale the intoxicating scent that fades as quickly as he grows out of the layette-size kimono... Are these the moments of wonder and awe that fortify us for the hard encounters of parenting, the times when you are reminded that a child doesn't come with an instruction manual?

One of these hard times happened on my son Tim's 21st birthday. I was unable to be home for the planned birthday celebration. As a certified nurse-midwife, I had been called to the hospital to attend a mom in labor. Tim came out to bring me some of his birthday dinner and cake. We sat in the call room and talked. He said he was feeling torn because it didn't look like the two most important women in his life would see eye to eye. He was thinking about moving in with his girlfriend, Anna, as he finished his undergraduate studies. He knew that I would not approve. Was he willing to make a decision that could tear the very fabric of our family?

That birthday was eight years ago. He did move in with her. While he was there, despite his frequent invitations to visit their apartment, Tim seemed to understand that in acquiescing to a visit, I would also be condoning their behavior. It was a very long year that followed, filled with worry and prayer. Both Tim and Anna were welcome in our home, but my son knew that I felt his living arrangement was a scandal to his younger siblings who were not able to go to the apartment either. Whatever the reasons, Tim and Anna broke off their relationship and he moved home with his 80 lb. American bulldog. What actually surprised me was his assumption that he felt there would be no question he could move back. He intuitively knew that our family home, as our family love, is a place of unconditional nurturing.

Mary Dahl Maher

"Human beings are the only creatures on earth that allow their children to come back home."
—Bill Cosby

Love Notes

As my children were growing up, I found many notes on my pillow when I went to bed. It became a fun way for my children, particularly Erica, to communicate with me. Recently I found a note she had written to me when she was in middle school: "Dear Mom, I got a start on my poem. Will you help me from 2:45 or 3:00 until 3:30?"

I smiled as I read it. Erica is now 28; I realize how that note expressed so accurately who she is today—organized and exact. Erica asked for help because she was not quite confident in her abilities and she wanted to do things well. She still wants to do things well but has gained more experience and confidence. I feel lucky that I was there to help her as she grew.

For Mother's Day at the end of her freshman year in college, Erica made me a book. In it are pictures of many things she was grateful for that I had been a part of or we had shared together. She had pictures of the goofy, silly Erica and the ridiculous, funny me that we had laughed about. She had pictures of uniquely shaped birthday cakes lovingly made and prom dresses carefully sewn. There were photos of vacations, Halloween costumes, Girl Scout sleepovers and at the end a picture of Erica on the phone. She wrote, "Thank you for getting me through my first year of college, for listening to me on the phone." It took me many years of trying to offer advice before I realized that my job was to listen, to support by just being on the other end of the phone.

Patricia Bertucci

Play Group

Earl showed up at my house one Thursday morning at 9 AM for our children's play group. He was standing in for his wife, Maria. The three boys and two girls were only three years old so they made a mess and did not really play "together." Earl's comment at seeing this interaction for the first time was that they played "side by side." How right he was! But from this chaotic beginning, the play group provided rich opportunities for growth and nurturing.

Those three-year-olds are now 22. They still talk of the time in play group that we rode the city bus downtown for lunch around Christmas. The little ones were all bundled up and so excited to ride in the back of the big bus. Then there was the time we took them bumper bowling. We learned songs, played games, read books and enjoyed time together—moms and kids.

While the play group only lasted two years, until they entered kindergarten, the kids still wanted to do things together and so did the moms. So we started two traditions. In the summer all five families went to Stony Brook State Park on a Sunday. We would leave home at about 8:30 in the morning; take breakfast and lunch food, bathing suits, hiking shoes, baseball bats and mitts. After a day of hiking the gorge, playing baseball, swimming and eating we would pack up and on the way home stop to eat at our favorite family diner, Tom Wahl's. We always got all the children—a total of 17 if they were all there—together for a picture.

In the fall we would make Christmas and Hanukah gifts on a Sunday afternoon. Over the years we sewed aprons, baked cookies, created Christmas trees and candleholders from wood. After the creating was finished, we had a potluck supper. After all these years, we still get together and support each other.

Patricia Bertucci

We've got this gift of love, but love is like a precious plant. You can't just accept it and leave it in the cupboard or just think it's going to get on by itself. You've got to keep watering it. You've got to really look after it and nurture it.

—John Lennon

Extended Family Love

Thanksgiving dinner at Grandma's and Pa's when I was growing up meant crisp white table linens, small candles of turkeys or pilgrims at each child's place, and delicious aromas that filled their upstairs flat. The women bustled in the kitchen outfitted in their Sunday best, adorned with homemade aprons while the men sat in the living room. Steamy kitchen windows reflected the warmth of hearth and home, surrounded as we were with happy chatter and the loving attention of extended family. This warmth still leaves its imprint on my memory today.

That's why when my children were small, we traveled to Rochester and Buffalo for Thanksgiving and Christmas, a long six or seven hour drive. We generally prepared for and celebrated Christmas in three different places and then drove home. It was a very large dose of family life, filled with tensions, dynamics and drama that often left me in a puddle of tears from exhaustion. But I never thought twice—family was what the holidays were all about.

Now that my children are grown I've wondered why we made it so hard on ourselves. My daughter recently showed me the answer. While on a family vacation, Anna, who is almost 30, wanted to cook a birthday meal in celebration of her Dad's 60th birthday. She lives on the West Coast, far from the rest of us. Nonetheless, she contacted two of the aunties, suggested dishes and organized all the details for dinner for 12. Then she and her boyfriend, Jason, flew in to cook the rest and laid it all on the table, hot and delicious, with the precision and ease of gourmet chefs. This was a new and surprising role-reversal. I felt so pampered and it melted her dad's heart.

Later, I asked her if she felt her extended family provided nurture and support. She replied, "Well, I've never known anything different. But extended family is my favorite part of the holidays—just having a lot of family around. I can always go to the store with an aunt. There's always something to do. I get to play with my younger cousins who I don't get to see the rest of the year. And I love the special meals with the ritual grace, toasts and lots of people. Big meals with lots of family are the holidays—the bigger the better!"

Suzanne Shady

"There are only two lasting bequests we can hope to give our children. One of these is roots, the other, wings."

—Hodding Carter

The Circle of Life

My father died of skin cancer at the age of 36. I was five. For the next six and a half years, our little family consisted of my mother, my older brother Louie, and me. We did everything together. Even though I never had a chance to know my father, my mother was everything that my brother and I needed.

When my brother was ten and I was eight, he enrolled for a week-long Boy Scout camping trip. For the first time, my family was separated. In an effort to make sure that I would miss Louie as little as possible, my mother insisted that we would spend every moment together. We had lunch dates, saw a movie, and even got dressed up and went shopping in downtown Cleveland. Through this, she showed me how important I was in her life.

My mother set high standards for my brother and me. Absolutely no fighting or even harsh words were allowed in our home. I remember her saying, "You're all I have." As my brother and I grew older, we began to ask, "But what about Grammy?" Her instant response was, "Grammy is my mother, but you are my children and my life." Whenever I needed her, she was always there—my mother, my friend, and my confidante.

As time wore on, our family changed. My mother got remarried to an old friend who was also widowed. I had to learn to adapt to a father and three new siblings. Six years later, I chose to attend a college far from home. After college, I married and began my own family. *My* children became *my* life. Despite the distance, I still knew that my mother was there for me. My siblings and I had all moved far away and my mother found herself caring for my second father by herself. She and I would often chat about our ever-evolving responsibilities. After my father died, our phone conversations changed yet again. I found that as my children became more independent, my mother became more dependent upon me.

I drove to Ohio to be with my mother when she was hospitalized for a severe case of pneumonia. When she seemed better, I returned home and she went back to her apartment with an armful of new prescriptions. A few days later, I received an alarming phone call. She had been taking two heart medications at the same time, resulting in serious heart arrhythmia. After my initial panic, I realized that she was starting to become forgetful and confused. She asked that I visit more often.

After numerous other hospitalizations, it became clear that my mother needed full-time care in a nursing home. I made the first of what would become many visits to Ohio. One weekend a month seemed like a small sacrifice for all she'd done for me. For two and a half years, I packed up some clothes, her small dog that had become one of my responsibilities, and often one of my own children, and began the five hour drive.

During these monthly visits, I performed countless errands that she could not do alone such as going to the grocery store and library. What proved to be the most challenging was when she wanted to come with me. From the oxygen tank to the dog, along with the two hours it took to get ready, a simple ride in the car became a logistical nightmare. Even when I wasn't there, she knew that she could depend on me for any of her basic needs. After a day at work, I would return home to an answering machine full of messages from my mother, asking for everything from tissues to a mirror to hang on the wall. Phone conversations with her became a part of my daily schedule, especially as she became more confused and needed more encouragement.

My mother passed away in April of 2008. She helped me understand that motherhood is more than the nurturing that mothers give to their children: it includes the nurturing that children offer their parents as they grow older.

Elizabeth O'Toole

Socialization

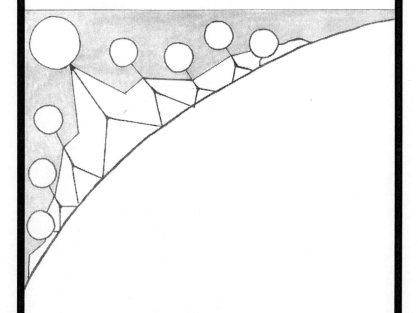

Learning to Live
With Others

3

"Home is the place where boys and girls first learn how to limit their wishes, abide by rules, and consider the rights and needs of others."
—Sidonie Gruenberg

3

Socialization

Learning to Live With Others

Have you ever noticed babies while you were in church or in line at the grocery store? They peek over their parent's shoulder at those behind them, sometimes with a shy smile, sometimes trying to engage the stranger by reaching out.

We humans are social beings. Our children start out curious about others, observing and interacting from the safety of our warm embrace. In what is often a very short time, perhaps only a couple of months, many children spend most of their day away from home and parents and in the company of a larger group.

One of the overriding desires we have as mothers is that our children will be able to get along with others on their journey to adulthood and independence. They have to be able to interact with others in a positive manner in order to be successful and contributing members of the greater society.

As a teacher, I found it interesting to see differences in students' abilities to share, work cooperatively, be truthful, and take responsibility. I found it challenging to try to assist those who had difficulty following classroom rules or getting along with others and who appeared to enjoy disrupting the learning environment.

As mothers we are our children's first teachers. Children need guidance and support as they navigate their expanding world of school and community. We need to give them important tools to live with others such as teaching them manners, how to understand and cope with their feelings and learning to accept limits and boundaries. For a mother of young children, it can be as narrow as easing a shy child into a neighborhood ball game or a new school. Or teaching how best to handle a bully or how to accept someone who is different from ourselves. As the children get older and outside influences begin to intrude into their lives, we need to help them learn to navigate new experiences and stand up for themselves. We also want our children to recognize goodness in those around them and to know how to give and receive graciously. Throughout their childhoods, our expectations of them, clearly stated, will have a profound effect on their accomplishments.   Our acknowledgement of their accomplishments will instill in them feelings of worth and purpose, contributing to their future success.

Sheila Roney

Magic Words

When Sarah was little, my husband and I worked to help her learn manners. As we attempted to teach her when to say "Please and Thank You" and when to share, we told her that "Please, Thank You and Share" were magic words. When she forgot to say them or was struggling to share, we would calmly remind her, "What are the magic words?"

On a trip to Toronto when Sarah was 2½ we stayed with friends. Dinner was an elegant affair and when Sarah was given some food she said, "Thank you." When she did not get a response from the hostess, Sarah turned to me and whispered, "She didn't say 'You're welcome'!" We've laughed frequently about that story but I'm glad that she was taking her manners very seriously!

Patricia Bertucci

"I was learning to live with others every day—I had 3 siblings. We played together all the time, and we also played with neighborhood kids. I think we learned a lot from those times, and it's good that we weren't always closely supervised and monitored—we needed to learn how to work things out on our own."

—Patricia's daughter Sarah Bertucci, 32 years old

No, Mine!

After my first baby was born, I was able to stay at home and not return to my teaching position. There were a few other stay-at-home moms in my neighborhood and as our children and families grew, we would take turns having "play group" at each others' houses. We felt our children needed the experience of being with other children to learn how to play, share, and generally get along with others.

My children each had something that was their favorite—a blanket, a doll, a stuffed animal—that was always within reach. When other children would try to use one of these beloved items, tempers could flare. Refrains of "Mine!"…"No Mine!" echoed back and forth. I thought I was teaching my children the concept of sharing by insisting they allow others to use these things. This approach left us all unhappy.

Fortunately, I came upon a suggestion in a magazine. The article stated we all have possessions that are important to us which we may not want to lend, and children are no different. I had my children put their one or two precious items in a safe place until friends went home. They were expected to share the rest of their play things. Problem solved.

Sheila Roney

"Children require guidance and sympathy far more than instruction."

—Anne Sullivan

Alex's Art Work

Alex, our 2 ½ year-old grandson, was spending the day with "Pa" and me. I was trying to have him draw with washable markers on a white board, but it was a dismal failure. The colors ended up on his face, shirt, and the carpet. When Mary Clare, a special education teacher and our youngest daughter, came by, she said she was going to color with Alex. "No," I warned her, "those markers just made a terrible mess."

She sat on the floor with Alex and took a marker out of the package. "Does the marker go here?" she asked, putting it on his nose.

"NO!" he said.

"Does it go here?" she asked, putting it on his ear.

"NO!" he said.

So it went as she tried other ridiculous places for a marker to go. Finally, she put it on the white board and asked, "Does it go here?"

"YES!"

"And does it go here?" she questioned, putting the marker back in the package.

"YES!"

They proceeded to have a very nice time coloring.

Diane Knittle

The Shy Little Girl

My daughter Anna was a timid little girl. At home she was cheery and talkative, but in social situations she often hung back and hid her face in my clothes. At the same time, she possessed an iron will that confounded her parents. Born into a family of gregarious extroverts, she and her parents had to make adjustments over the years.

One setting where this was particularly challenging was at church on Sunday. We belonged to a very large congregation and there were many new faces every week. One part of our worship service is extending a Sign of Peace to your neighbor, which entails shaking hands or giving a family member an embrace with a few words. Anna would ignore any friendly overtures, even from children. I was perplexed and felt a twinge of embarrassment at her response, which seemed both anti-social and rude. Coaxing was for naught. One Sunday we talked about it on the way home. My husband and I explained to Anna what the Sign of Peace is, why it's done, and how people would feel if she offered it to them. We encouraged her to participate.

Gradually, she did respond, in her own way, to a few people and at her own pace. The next Sunday Anna put out a tentative hand and spoke softly to those around her. She got such a warm response that soon she was happily participating in this activity along with everyone else. What we learned was that this was her sweet, shy personality, which we needed to respect, along with her unique way of responding to life. With this insight, it mattered less to us that she didn't respond warmly to a new friend, or needed an adult to help her feel secure in new situations. We began to understand her temperament and her needs.

This experience also helped us see that we needed to teach our children basic social skills that we took for granted. It set the stage for training to look at the person talking to you, speak so they can hear you, shake their hand, *smile*, etc., which our children sometimes responded positively to and sometimes did not.

Over the years Anna continued to be shy in new social situations. But as she grew up, she came into her own and now as an adult meets those challenges with grace and skill in spite of her shy temperament. It is clear to us that our very simple efforts to guide and encourage her made a difference.

Suzanne Shady

"Nothing you do for children is ever wasted. They seem not to notice us, hovering, averting our eyes, and they seldom offer thanks, but what we do for them is never wasted."

—Garrison Keillor

Home Base

It was our sixth move in six years of marriage. We were tired, we were hot, and it was August. My oldest daughter, Kim, was starting kindergarten in a week and she did not want to leave my side. Several times during the course of move-in day, we collided; my patience was running thin. I was becoming desperate about her well-being.

In our many trips from the moving van to the house, we saw and heard a large group of kids playing in our cul-de-sac. As we unloaded our belongings, we saw that in their game of kickball, our driveway was home plate. My husband realized that it would be to our advantage if Kim was playing outside. He also knew it would be a good chance for her to make new friends. He piggy-backed her out to our new front yard and introduced her to the neighborhood.

He set her down in the middle of the game and they watched together until a break in the game. "Hi, I'm Mr. O'Toole and this is Kim," he said to our pint-sized neighbors, "Can she play with you?" The kids were thrilled that the girl who lived at home base wanted to be their friend. For Kim, this broke the ice and she quickly became part of the neighborhood gang. When she started school three weeks later she found a host of friendly faces who helped ease her transition into her new school just like they had in the neighborhood.

Elizabeth O'Toole

Coping with Change

Moving from one community to another is a big change, especially for children. When Anna was almost five, we left a great neighborhood with lots of friends in Virginia and moved to New Jersey. Anna started in a new kindergarten class in mid-February. She was anxious about the change. Thankfully her fears were allayed by a warm teacher and nurturing atmosphere. The first week she was very excited—being the 'new girl' meant lots of attention and new friends—but soon she found herself ignored when established friendships were resumed. The following week I got an apologetic phone call from the teacher who said that a few boys had teased Anna, pushed her down, which had given her a bloody nose.

When I picked Anna up from school that day she climbed into the front seat of the car with a very sad face. She looked so vulnerable and small wrapped in the big seat belt as she tearfully poured out her story. She lamented having no friends, nobody to play with and described the mean boys who teased and pulled her hair until she fell. Mama-bear instincts welling up, I searched for what to say. We talked about what happens when you are the new kid and how it takes time to make friends. I remembered how timid she could be and her tendency to squeal and take offence—an easy target for bullies. So I told her if it happened again she should lower her voice and tell them loudly, "Stop that! I don't like it!" We even practiced a few times.

Then I reminded her of one of her story books, *The 329ʰ Friend*. Emery Raccoon had been lonely and invited 328 new friends to lunch, but nobody was listening to him because they were so busy having fun. So Emery decided to go inside and entertain himself; he realized that he could be his own good friend. In the end everyone got to know each other and had a fun time. I told her for now she would have to be her own good friend too and we could invite some children over to our house. This seemed to provide a measure of comfort. Thankfully, Anna remembered the story and said with a bit of cheer, "You mean Emery had to be his own best friend?"

Suzanne Shady

Bully Boy

When my third daughter was in elementary school there was a boy who bullied her. Though it never became physical, he called her names, made rude comments, and made fun of her. At the end of the day she would run home from the bus in tears, sobbing out her story of that day's incident. My philosophy was to let my daughter and this bully take care of the situation themselves, even though it was most painful as a mother to hear her complaints. The response I gave after much consideration was that he must feel bad about himself. I gave her hug after hug and said that this bullying behavior reflected his wounded feelings.

The class graduated from elementary, middle and high school. The summer of their second year of university, the class had a reunion which my daughter and the bullyboy attended. To our surprise, the boy apologized to my daughter for his hurtful behavior towards her.

There are lessons to be learned through adversity. My daughter learned to cope with difficulty, hold her own, ignore what she could, speak up for herself and seek support from family and friends. Looking back, she could see the inappropriate behavior of someone who was having difficulty making friends because of poor self esteem. In the end she was vindicated because she had taken the high road and the boy knew it. My guess is he learned a few lessons as well.

Patricia Costigan

No!

When Peter was finally old enough to shower by himself, his sisters, father and I would listen to him sing in the shower. We'd smile and hope that he would follow in the footsteps of his sisters and join the children's choir at church. He did.

One fall the choir director was able to get discount tickets for the Harlem Boys' Choir, which was going to perform at the Eastman Theater in Rochester, NY. I asked Peter if he'd like to go and he said yes, so I purchased tickets for him, two of his sisters and myself. His father wasn't interested.

The Sunday afternoon of the concert found us all getting ready to go. Eight-year-old Peter had pants on with a hole in the knee so I asked him to change them. He said, "No." I was shocked and said that he could pick his pants, but they could not have a hole in them. Again, he said, "No." By that point, I was exasperated. I desperately wanted Peter to have the opportunity to hear the choir sing, to enjoy the concert with us, but I also knew he needed to change those pants. I told him that unless he changed the pants, he would not go to the concert, but would stay home in his room. He would not bother his father. And he would need to do chores for me in order to earn the money to pay for the ticket he chose not to use. He still would not change the pants, so the girls and I left for the concert without him.

On the entire drive to the Eastman Theater, I fretted, for I had really wanted Peter to hear the boys sing. I had wanted us to spend the time together. However, what I wanted did not happen that Sunday afternoon. The concert was amazing though it took me a while to relax and enjoy it. Peter took me seriously and did stay in his room. He also did go back to singing in the shower, but that day we both learned the pain involved in saying "No."

Patricia Bertucci

"The gem cannot be polished without friction nor man perfected without trials."

—Chinese Proverb

Come-unity Center

We lived in a three story, five bedroom house in 'Apple Country,' New York State. There were many orchards: sweet and sour cherry orchards, but mostly apple orchards. Cherries were picked in late July and early August. Apples began in late August and continued until late October. The fruit was harvested by migrant workers. They came up from the south in July and stayed until the harvesting was over. They travelled light, and often did not have adequate clothing. Picking fruit by hand was slow and tedious and dirty. Dirty because of the various sprays that were used to kill insect pests.

A local group of concerned residents opened up a used clothing store called THE COME-UNITY CENTER. It's still there. Fannie Mae, who had been a migrant, became the coordinator. I volunteered and brought our youngest daughter, Juanita, with me. She was a pre-schooler who loved to have stories read to her; with seven older brothers and sisters there was usually someone available. Juanita would take a book off the shelf and go sit on Fannie Mae's lap and ask her to read the story. Fanny Mae did not know how to read, but she made up a story to match the pictures.

That same year, several volunteers came to the area to provide better services for migrant workers. They were part of VISTA (Volunteers in Service to America), a forerunner of AMERICORPS. Their services included literacy programs and Fannie Mae took advantage of this. Two young VISTA women lived with us for a month while they were in training and we became acquainted with all of the volunteers. It became known that on Tuesday I baked eight loaves of bread. So by late Tuesday afternoon about the time my older children got off the school bus, the volunteers would drop by to visit. Between them and my children coming home from school those eight loaves shrank to six within a matter of minutes.

Juanita, who was at home with me during the day, was the one who had the most interaction with members of the Center and the Volunteers. She remembers the happiness and the fun she had being part of this caring community. These early experiences helped her develop an ability to appreciate people of diverse racial and ethnic backgrounds. This attitude has benefitted her in her career as a marine biologist conducting research around the world.

Patricia Urban

As adults we must ask more of our children
then they know how to ask of themselves.
What can we do to foster their open-hearted hopefulness,
engage their need to collaborate, be an incentive to utilize
their natural competency and compassion?
(We can) show them ways they can connect, reach out,
weave themselves into the web of relationships
that is called community.

—Dawna Markova

A Beautiful Day in the Neighborhood

When we moved into our new house, it was a cold, dreary and dark December day. The boxes were stacked throughout the downstairs with narrow paths which the children used as a maze to run through. The doorbell rang. Thinking it might be the utilities representative to turn on the heat, my husband went to the door and I heard him engaging in social banter with a woman. He came back and asked me if we were doing anything Thursday night. I couldn't think that we'd be doing anything between that day and Christmas except unpacking boxes and trying to make the house habitable before our seventh baby's expected arrival date just one month away. He went back to the front entryway and returned quickly with a look on his face that registered an odd combination of amusement and consternation. "That was the woman who lives across the street. She's arranging a potluck to welcome us to the neighborhood."

I responded that it was a nice gesture and asked if he knew whose house we'd be going to and hoped he'd told her we had six children so we wouldn't be able to stay late. My gregarious husband chuckled, anticipating my shocked response that we were going to be the hosts as well as the guests! I was too worn out to offer any resistance.

The planned day arrived and we tried to clear an area to sit down on some of the sturdier boxes. This was our fourth move in four years and we had a total of one couch and four chairs. Since I hadn't planned on being the hostess, I thought, a little too smugly, that people would be less likely to stay late if they weren't comfortable.

The evening was a reversal of my expectations. In addition to the 80-something matriarch who spear-headed the repast, two other families joined us. "Grandma Collins" was a little embarrassed at the poor showing but explained that, with only two days notice during the busy Christmas holiday season, others sent their regrets. It was a perfect welcome. With just the right amount of deference, our new neighbors came in and took over. Dennis helped us hook up the stove so Betsy could keep the meatballs warm while the pasta boiled. Over homemade pie made with frozen rasp-berries picked from their own backyard, Barb and Bob shared the story of their move to Rochester so many years before. Our daughters made two new friends while the children occupied themselves with hide and seek.

We all learned that being a good neighbor sometimes requires feeling a little awkward as we step out of our per-sonal comfort zone to meet the other. The reward comes in feeling part of a community. Although few of our neighbors are close friends, we know every face by name and are secure in the knowledge that we can depend on one another in very old-fashioned neighborly ways. We were fortunate to find and move into a city neighbor-hood where folks actively valued civic engagement and showed us what it meant to be a good neighbor.

Mary Dahl Maher

Schedule A and Schedule B

"We haven't been doing our job," said my husband. Our seven-year-old daughter had been told that before she could go out and play she had to put away her laundry. As Bill and I looked at the pile of her washed and folded laundry that she had strewn across her bedroom, we knew that something had to change. Her five-year-old sibling was no better.

Bill told me to pray and think about a way to incorporate the children into the household chores. He explained to them, after we had called them inside, that being a family means everyone pitching in to make life manageable for all.

Thus was born "Schedule A and Schedule B" which were posted on the refrigerator. Each "schedule" differed and listed five chores, taking no longer than ten to fifteen minutes. The children could do one chore a day or they could choose to do all five on Saturday morning. In any case, whatever was not done by Saturday had to be done before they could play. At first the chores were simple: put away laundry, wash out the bathroom sink, and dust the tables in the living room. As time went by and they matured the jobs grew appropriately: iron two of Dad's shirts, fold a load of laundry, and clean the tub. Each week the children would switch "schedules" so that the chores did not become too monotonous.

Now married with families of their own, their wives and husbands thank us for the training we gave our children in family cooperation.

Diane Knittle

Out of the Mouths of Babes

Mari was my 6th child in 9 years to go through high school and I knew all the trouble that teens were capable of getting into. She was 15 and asking yet again for another opportunity to find that trouble. All she really wanted to do was to go out with her friends and I really didn't want her to go. I had no specific reason but was still very reluctant to give her permission. Steve, at 17 the only sibling and fellow high school student left at home with her, stopped me as I began my tiresome tirade.

He told me to stop yelling at her as if she had done something wrong. I told him that I wasn't yelling, but he insisted I was being too hard on her. He said that I'd yelled at him but he'd deserved it, and that I should wait until she did something wrong to get angry. I looked at Mari and asked if she thought I was yelling and she nodded. I paused for a moment and then apologized to her and told her that from that moment on there would be a new set of rules.

I told them that if they wanted to do something with their buddies, they had to have the answers to all the questions they knew I would ask before they came to me for permission. If I asked a question and there was no information forthcoming, then my answer would be an automatic no. That made them responsible to have a whole plan in place before they approached me. Sometimes the answer was still no. Friday night midnight bowling...I don't think so! But for the most part it was an excellent system. They became organized problem solvers for their own social lives and there was no more yelling on my part.

Jo Ann Figueiredo

Lessons with Love

Our church asks members to host homeless families for a week at a time. On one occasion there was a beautiful family with a teenage son and a three-year-old daughter who had recently moved to our country. The children were quite well behaved. The dad was a sturdy, gregarious man whose wife was reserved and lovely.

During the week of their stay, this family taught us some valuable lessons. The children showed great respect for their parents. I observed the little girl trying to convince her mother to give her something. The mother gently said, "No," and continued to say "no" firmly and kindly until the little girl stopped asking. Each time the mother responded to her daughter with the same gentle, firm "no." If the daughter was particularly adamant, the father stepped in and supported his wife. The older son already knew what his younger sister was learning: Mom and Dad mean what they say, so it is no use to argue with them.

They also showed us with their closeness and love for each other, that "home" was found in the circle of their family. The positive attitude of the father in this difficult situation was reflected in his children. They were grateful for the little that they had and grateful to those who helped them. We learned some beautiful lessons in attitude, respect and how to care for one another.

Patricia Costigan

Learning Social Skills through Sports

Recently I had a conversation with Kate, 28, about the choices we, her parents, had made for her during her childhood. She said that one thing she was very happy we had done was to expose her and her siblings to a lot of different things and people. Having brought our children up in the same middle class suburb that I had grown up in, I was very surprised to hear her say that.

We never hesitated to put them into new situations, she explained. We found interesting programs for them to join, such as tennis with inner city children and theater camp at the local college. We didn't just keep them with school friends but were open to teams and programs where we ourselves knew no one. We sent them to a Presbyterian day camp for at least ten years and joined the local Jewish Community Center to take advantage of a great basketball program every winter.

Of course the kids were never alone; there was always a sibling close by participating in another age group. Because I had a friend who worked at a small urban YMCA I applied for a job there. I became a nursery school teacher in the "Y" program and my kids were able to take swimming lessons and participate in other activities because of that. The older three even participated on a swim team for two years and played "T" ball on "Y" based teams. We met all kinds of people there.

As the kids got older and played sports at ever more competitive levels, we sometimes moved them from team to team always looking for what we felt was best for them. Emily played on our local travel soccer team and the coach was not very nice. At the time she had a pair of soccer cleats that were white. She was very pigeon toed and shoes that fit well were hard to come by. We were happy to have found these shoes. One day the coach made fun of her in front of the team saying that no real soccer players wore white cleats. Other issues came up over the course of the season and we decided that she would be better off finding another team for the following year. Our suburb refused to allow a second team in that age group so we went to the neighboring suburb where there was a soccer program that allowed her dad to start up a new team. This team has just completed its 12th year together.

According to Kate, while I thought the kids were just playing games and learning to win and lose graciously and how to be good team members they were also receiving grounding in how to face the world. They learned how to meet people they might otherwise never encounter, how to be open to new experiences and how to move on from an uncomfortable situation to one that was just right for them—all good skills for getting on in life.

Jo Ann Figueiredo

VALUES

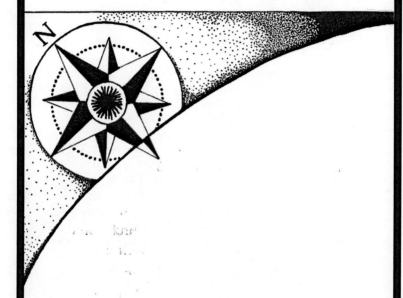

A Moral Compass for
Life's Journey

4

> *"The walks and talks we have with our two-year-olds in red boots have a great deal to do with the values they will cherish as adults."*
> Edith F. Hunter

4

Values

A Moral Compass for Life's Journey

It was a blustery day in February, 1979, and I remember it as if it were yesterday. My husband gingerly carried our brand new daughter into the house, set her down on the coffee table in the living room, car seat and all, looked at me, and said, "Now what do we do?" Truth be told, I was just as clueless and a little frightened.

I've learned a lot since that moment. However the responsibility of bringing up a value-filled human being still seems to be the most daunting task of a parent.

How do you help someone grow that dimension of self that will resonate from their core and that will help them use their skills in a personally and socially responsible way when they are grown?

There is a certain elusive quality when the word values is mentioned just as our parenting skills may also be elusive at the very start of our journey as parents. To enable a child to function is one thing, but to help them be the best person they can be and to treat others with respect day in and day out is the true goal. We need to remember that they will grow up to make their own choices, but we will want to rest easy knowing we have given them the moral compass that will guide them in their decision making.

We are all born with unknown depths of potential. How exactly are values or a value-based life realized from that potential? The best I can figure out is that values happen while the mundane things of life are taking place. The strength of our children's characters may be a direct reflection not only of the strength of our voice and authority in our roles as nurturer and educator, but also of the example we have set in the way we have conducted ourselves as we have gone about our lives. Our child will imitate us as we imitated our parents.

How do we steer our child towards those values that we cherish? Our children are being brought up in a world of varied societal norms which are attractive and misleading. We need to do the best we can to make sure they recognize what we hold dear. We have to share what we know to be the building blocks of good character by making consistent moral choices that express our priorities. High standards of sexual and ethical morality, integrity, tolerance, compassion, and the courage to live by the standards we have set for ourselves are some of the lessons that form the challenge that lies ahead for all parents. In other words, we must show them exactly what we want them to be by our behavior day after day, every day. We are their support and their guide into adulthood.

While the thought seems daunting—raising a child with values that will be a moral compass through all of life—our view from the empty nest is reassuring. Raising children with moral values is similar to knitting a sweater—the love, effort and attention that goes into it pays off. There may be a dropped stitch here or there, one may discover a mistake and have to rework an entire row and different yarns may be woven into the whole, but in the end, the beautiful sweater pattern is what stands out.

Of course, like all of life, there are no guarantees—the challenges of modern society impact us all, often painfully. Each and every child is unique, with the freedom to make his/her own choices. And, as parents, we have our strengths and weaknesses and none of us came from perfect families. But what we nine moms see, looking at our collective 43 children is that while they may live out their values very differently, they are good people. They are honest, live with integrity, and reach out to others and the community to make a difference. As moms we still worry for them, cringe over their mistakes or problems, but rejoice in who they are becoming. Each child brought lots of opportunity for teaching, testing and bring-you-to-your-knees challenge. Nothing quite prepares you. But we learned what is required is an open heart, the willingness to respond and courage—because to act on one's values often means stepping away from the crowd.

Naturally, as parents, we took on this task as a labor of love. We wanted to shape and guide these special little lives. But we struggled! It was a process of growth for all of us. We were sometimes surprised at the results which often aren't apparent for years. Now with our children grown, we see that the expectations that we held for them, and the values we tried to model, had an impact. As each child has faced life's challenges these strong values have helped them stay the course.

Jo Ann Figueiredo

The Coat

When Brian was about 12, his dad, Bob, went to school to give him a ride home. It was a cold, blustery day, and I had an after-school snack ready and waiting for him and his sisters.

As soon as Brian and Bob arrived home, they began to look for an old jacket of Bob's that he didn't wear much anymore. While they were searching, Bob told me that as they were driving home, Brian spotted a boy bigger than he, walking home without a jacket. Brian did not know him but had seen him before without a coat. This really bothered Brian, and he asked Bob if he had a jacket that they could give to the boy.

Eventually they found it, went back out, and gave the boy the coat. At first he did not want to take it, but Brian was so earnest about it that he finally accepted it.

I don't remember if the "coatless boy" was seen or mentioned again, but on that day our family put into action one of our values: Treat others as you would like to be treated.

Sheila Roney

Princess

It was September of 1993 and my daughter Sara was heading off to high school for the first time. She was going to the local all-girls Catholic school, and she had many things to think about. There was a homeroom full of strangers waiting for her and a new locker and a combination lock to memorize. There was a daunting schedule to follow, teacher upon teacher to meet. The concerns were endless.

The one thing she was confident about was her outfit for the first day of school. Her brand new uniform hung primly in her closet ready for the next four years of her life but today, just for this day, she could wear dress-up, or was it dress-down, no matter, she had the killer outfit, and she could hardly wait to wear it.

Oblivious to the bustle around her as the whole household prepared for the first day of the new school year, she appeared in the kitchen, hoisted her brand new backpack on her shoulder and prepared to meet the day. What she met instead was the horrified look on my face. I was standing at the kitchen counter awash in breakfast debris and lunch bags. Sara immediately stopped when she saw me. She knew something was wrong, but what could it be?

Sara was a talkative and friendly girl who had begun to develop her own approach to life and increasingly was trying to make more of her own decisions. I was totally unprepared for the vision of my daughter in her outfit.

I knew of the conservative nature of Sara's new high school, as I had also attended there as a teen, and I remembered the nuns, their strict rules and their distaste for anything approaching current fashion. I felt that Sara would be setting herself up for unwanted attention on Day One by entering the school in her rather revealing blouse. I also knew that first impressions were extremely important and that Sara did not realize that she might be seen as a brazen girl without many thoughts in her head, even though she was neither of those things.

There was an immediate collision of Sara's expectations and my protestations. She told me that she and her best friend were dressing alike and had decided on this outfit. With a sinking heart I told her that she could not leave the house as dressed. The poor bewildered Sara, receiving my undivided attention for the first time that morning, became angry and defensive. I stood my ground trying to explain the problem, but there was no time for discussion. When Sara left for school, she was still resentful that her grand plan had been thwarted and I, in turn, was sad that such a big day for her had been tarnished.

The years went by and the incident of the blouse was long forgotten. Then one day Sara, now grown up and out of college, stopped me in my tracks with a sweet comment. Once again she had my complete and undivided attention as she calmly, almost offhandedly, said that she was glad that she had not worn that particular shirt to school that day because it would have sent the wrong message to the teachers about who she was and how she wanted to be seen. She hugged me and thanked me for my motherly intervention. I hugged back and thanked her for telling me.

Jo Ann Figueiredo

"Maybe it's the job of parents to make age-old standards of behavior relevant in today's society and culture."
   —Jo Ann's daughter Marie Figueiredo, 17 years old

The Tao of Motherhood

If you hold to the Eternal in thought, word, and action
your children will return again and again to you.
Your children may not understand the depth of your
parenting until later. They may question your values and
say you are "weird" or not like other kids' parents.
They may say your life is boring or strange.
Never mind.
The wise are not caught up in appearances.
The way is at times boring in its simplicity.
Hold to it.
The superficial eventually repels.
That which is real attracts every good thing to it.

Vimala McClure (1997)

What's the Rating?

It was another tenth birthday party. The invitation to this one was informal; my son shared the details as told to him by the birthday boy. The party was to be at the child's home and would involve a sleep-over with a group of boys, pizza, birthday cake, ice-cream, and movies.

It was the last item, movies, which concerned me. Many of the television shows and movies had themes or situations which we felt were inappropriate for our children and we tried to monitor what they watched. Part of this was accomplished by limiting the amount of TV they viewed during the school week. We also made it clear that the movie rating was taken into consideration when determining which movies they would be allowed to watch.

As a result, it did not come as a surprise to my son when I asked if he knew what movies were planned and their ratings. Though he did not have all the details, he did know some scary videos were to be part of the night.

Needing more information, I called and spoke with the boy's dad. He verified the party plans and was honest in telling me a couple of the movies were rated R. In response I said that my son would be there for the early part of the celebration but would not stay to watch movies or spend the night and explained why.

Of course my son was disappointed. I was too, but for a different reason. It would have been easy for that dad to say he understood my concerns and they would find some other videos to watch so my son could be included, but he didn't.

Sheila Roney

Altar Serving 101

It was something you did if you lived in our house. As soon as you got old enough, you were trained to serve at mass at our local parish church. That's how it was for Joe when he was about 8 years old. He always served with his two older sisters who were already accomplished altar servers. They took charge when on duty and rarely asked any more of him than to occasionally follow their direction. He was very comfortable in his role and actually looked quite competent to the casual observer.

Then one morning Joe was officially the older altar server and his younger sister, Emily, newly trained, was on the altar with him. We watched as he made one misstep after the other, several times even being saved by Emily doing the right thing on her own. We realized that morning that Joe had somehow managed not to internalize any of the details of the job. He had literally dreamed away one full year of altar serving.

Miss Leonard, the exacting altar serving teacher was in attendance that morning. She always watched with a very critical eye from the pew and oftentimes had a comment or two to make to the servers at the end of mass. Even adults cringed at the sight of her bearing down on the poor servers.

At the end of mass as we waited for Joe and Emily to put out the candles we stopped to talk with some friends. When they saw Miss Leonard make a bee-line for Joe, they implored us to intervene to protect him from her wrath. We didn't interfere, feeling that maybe

Joe should hear whatever she had to say. She walked up to him, looked him in the eye and said, "Not good Joe, not good." That was all, no yelling or other demonstrations of adult frustration. Joe just blushed and hung his head. He was disappointed in himself.

No one else leaving the church probably even noticed the exchange but it had a profound effect on him. The next time he altar served he actually did the job as it was supposed to be done. He grew up a little that day and we inadvertently let that happen by trusting another adult, a teacher, to set an expectation for our child and to reinforce the expectation when it was needed.

Jo Ann Figueiredo

"If you want children to keep their feet on the ground, put some responsibility on their shoulders."
—Abigail Van Buren

I Need It!

The Star-Wars spaceship cost $25 at K-Mart. "I need it. Everyone has one," said 9-year-old Michael. Gathered for dinner at our kitchen table, my husband responded, "Need it, Mike? What is the difference between 'need' and 'want'?"

Michael's silence spoke volumes. You could almost hear his thoughts, "Oh, no. This doesn't sound good."

The other children began to volunteer answers: "We need love, a house to live in, food, something to wear, each other."

"So, Michael, you don't NEED the spaceship, do you? But if you *want* it, how can you earn the money to buy it?"

Five weeks later, after cutting many of the neighbors' lawns, Michael made his first-ever purchase with his hard-earned $25.

Diane Knittle

"Loving a child doesn't mean giving into all his whims; to love him is to bring out the best in him, to teach him to love what is difficult."

—Nadia Boulanger

Alicia and Charlie

I learned to have compassion for others from my parents who insisted that I do volunteer work while I was in high school. My work at an inner-city settlement house helped me choose to become a teacher. It also affected my decision to marry someone who showed care and concern for others.

As a teenager, our second child Andrea, worked a number of summers at Camp Silver Birch, a day camp run by the Sisters of Mercy. One summer she had fake Birkenstocks. When the sandals got wet, the dye colored her feet a blacky-blue, which made them look quite bruised. Alicia, one of the campers asked Andrea what had happened, so she created a crazy story of how I had run over her feet when backing the car out of the driveway. Imagine my surprise when I met Alicia and she said, "Oh, you're the one who ran over Andrea's feet." Andrea brought humor, compassion, and love into her relationship with the campers, especially Alicia and her younger brother Charlie.

Andrea met Alicia as a ten-year-old and twelve years later they still keep in touch. Over the years Alicia has sought advice from Andrea. Alicia lived with her mom when she was not in jail or in rehab for drug abuse. At other times Alicia lived with her grandfather. She took on the responsibility of caring for her younger siblings. When she had no other way to get laundry done and Andrea was away at college or in Boston working, Alicia would call me for help with her laundry. I would pick her up with her loads of dirty clothes and drop her off at the Laundromat with money and sometimes detergent.

When Alicia was in high school, she frequently had to attend summer school. Sometimes she would wake up late and call me to please give her a ride to school. With Alicia's dogged persistence, and support from Andrea and me, she graduated from high school—not a small feat considering her background. Alicia is now twenty-two and working in Atlanta. Unfortunately Andrea was not able to have as positive an effect on Charlie's life. He is now in jail, but writing to her. So she is providing hope for him and his future.

Patricia Bertucci

"Morality is like a roadmap for living...Moral roads also fork and that's why you need moral roadmaps: for choosing which fork to take on the road of life."
—Peter Kreeft

We grow morally as a consequence of learning how to be with others, how to behave in this world, a learning prompted by taking to heart whatever we have seen and heard. The child is a witness: the child is an ever attentive witness of grown-up morality—or lack thereof: the child looks and looks for cues as to how one ought to behave, and finds them galore as we parents and teachers go about our lives, making choices, addressing people, showing in action our rock bottom assumptions, desires, and values, and thereby telling those young observers much more than we realize.

—Robert Coles, *The Moral Intelligence of Children*

Family Gifts

Christmas 2006 brought some issues for family discussion. Now that our four children were all young adults, we had tried to simplify gift giving, but it had not been very successful. So their dad and I decided to have a family meeting. Family meetings had started when the children were young—some were productive, some were not. In the beginning, we parents were not very skilled at facilitating but we persevered with help from books like *How to Talk so Kids Will Listen and Listen so Kids Will Talk,* by Faber and Mazlish, and found the meetings valuable starting points to keep communication going.

At this meeting so many years into the process, we discussed the pros and cons of gift giving. One daughter's feelings were hurt by her older sister's suggestion to give no more gifts. She was very uncomfortable expressing her own desire to give special gifts. We spoke of being there for each other over the years and of the importance of honesty in relationships. At one point it was mentioned that Dad would always pick up any of his children if they called and asked, no matter what the circumstances. During this conversation Peter, our youngest, was asked his thoughts. He offered that when his friends drank too much alcohol, they would frequently call him for a ride. He said that friends asked him why he was willing to do that, and he said he figured it was something his sisters would do. I was touched to think that my quiet son would help his friends and that he would share that with us.

This discussion was an unexpected gift to us parents. We could see so clearly the results of our parenting. The many years of toil, anguish, and admonitions had borne fruit. Our efforts to instill values were reflected throughout the discussion that evening, and Peter's simple statement brought it all into focus. No final decisions were made regarding gift giving, but I saw the gift that came to all of us through our efforts to share honestly with one another through the years at family meetings.

Patricia Bertucci

The Bed-time Story

I was about seven, the age my mother was when both of her parents died. I was snuggled in my parents' bed with Mom and my two sisters, Maureen and Patty, who were then five and three. Mom was reading our nightly bedtime story. It was warm and cozy and I can still feel how deliciously special that time was with her. That year she read us two stories, which soon became my all-time favorites: *A Summer to Remember* by Erma M. Karoli, and *The Boxcar Children* by Gertrude Chandler Warner. Both described a child or children who faced tragedy and, through the goodness of others, found healing, happiness, and a new life. In a very real way these stories reflected my mother's own life and the values she held dear: nurturing her family, caring for the vulnerable, and creating a home.

I know now that those stories held great emotional import for my mother and that emotion was conveyed to me. Both of these stories have been formative in who I am and what I value. I've grown up committed to family and mothering. I continue to try to create a warm and inviting home. Professionally, I've worked with handicapped children and now work as a hospital chaplain. Most significantly, I love to read at bedtime and over the years always read to my children each night. It was a ritual that still speaks to me of intimacy and special closeness.

Suzanne Shady

"You may have tangible wealth untold, caskets of jewels and coffers of gold. Richer than I you will never be—I had a parent who read to me."

—Strickland Gillilan

Tattle Tale

My little brown-eyed son's third grade teacher called me to alert me to the fact that, although she appreciated his sincere desire to see that the right thing was always done, he was making enemies in the classroom by tattling. I sat down with him and explained how proud I was of him for learning to do the right thing. However, I told him, he needed to let the teacher take care of the children that were making bad choices because she was the authority figure in the classroom. He needed to just watch out for himself. I told him that if he wanted to be friends with his classmates he had to stop telling on them. He understood and said that he would mind his own business and let the teacher mind the business of the others.

The next day my little guy burst in the front door in tears. "I did it again, Mommy. I told on someone." I took him in my arms and said, "Honey, sometimes we do the thing we hate one more time and it shows us just how much we don't want to do it. Don't worry now. You will never do it again, I'm sure, because you see how bad it feels to tell on others." And he never did.

Diane Knittle

Service: Our Way of Life

I guess I just simply never thought about it. Service has always been such an important part of our lives. We are here on Earth to serve. My husband and I have served on countless boards and committees, as well as various ministries in our parish. In fact, even our careers serve the public. John is a volunteer firefighter in our town as well as a New York State fire instructor. I am the director of the Youth Services Section of the New York Library Association as well as the youth specialist at the local library.

On September 6, 2001, we drove our oldest daughter, Kimberly, to Iona College in New Rochelle, NY, to begin her studies. On September 11, 2001, the world as we knew it changed forever. Within hours, the Christian Brothers had the students praying and working with the Red Cross. Kimberly was deeply affected, as many of her friends were directly involved due to the close proximity of her campus to the city. One young man's father was killed as a New York City firefighter first responder.

Soon after, Kimberly joined Midnight Madness, a college organization that included students from several area campuses. This group bought as many meals as finances permitted from a local fast food restaurant, and then hand delivered them at midnight to the most dangerous streets of NYC. Their mission was to feed as many people as possible in a short period of time.

A few days after her first time doing this, she phoned me. My sweet, naïve, young daughter described what it felt like to meet homeless people face-to-face, to step over these people who actually lived on the street, and to put food in their hands. She broke down and cried. "I never really appreciated all of your volunteering but now I can't imagine my life without it," she said. I don't know who cried more during that phone call, Kim or mom.

Elizabeth O'Toole

"Children have never been very good at listening to their elders, but they have never failed to imitate them."

—James Baldwin

Transformers

The November sky was overcast and reflected my mood as I pondered how I would deal with the latest challenge of motherhood. The *Sears Wish Book* had arrived the previous month and my three sons had excitedly pored over the pages while eleven-year-old Christopher listed their desires on the order form. Oblivious to the great goings on, two-year-old Hannah danced around her brothers as they worked.

This catalog perusing was sowing the seeds of the second annual Christmas free-for-all, courtesy of my mother who had taken to spending three to four month periods living with us. She knew no limits when it came to pleasing her grandchildren. Busy with my everyday life of mothering and homemaking, I never thought she would send the order out before I had time to check.

Now, three weeks later, Grandma had gone home and the UPS man had just unloaded six very large boxes from Sears. I quickly inventoried the contents before the boys returned from school. Matchbox cars and Lincoln logs tumbled out first and were met with a nod. Then I could feel my heart drop as I came to three boxes of Transformers. A new, fad toy that looked like fancy racecars or spaceships but with a twist of the hand, pieces could be flipped to reveal the "menacing robot in disguise." I read the detailed story line on the boxes with dismay. How would my pacifist husband respond to the "Decepticon Robot," the Megatron whose tag line read "Lesser creatures are the playthings of my will"?

The tag line for the next one was no better—glorifying the intergalactic war of good vs. evil.

It was time for the boys to be home. I decided not to mention the exciting delivery until I was able to speak to my husband that evening. I didn't know which I dreaded more—the firm disapproval of my husband with his mother-in-law's latest extravagance or the disappointment of my children. I knew I would support my husband's fatherly wisdom but struggled to find a way to please both.

The boys arrived and the after school routine began to unfold. Christopher ran down the small apartment hall to get his sister's jacket. With the ESP that children sometimes demonstrate, he stopped in the master bedroom where the cardboard tower loomed tall and inviting. He knew these were gifts but he had placed the order and so felt justified in taking a peek. He sighed in disbelief as he saw the Transformers on top. His school buddies said they were already on back order and here he found every single model made. He and Grandma had scored! Too late, I walked in. Shutting the door behind me I sank on to the bed and looked into the excitement of big brown eyes.

"Mom, this is so incredible! We're going to have the best gifts ever! Grandma is amazing!" (*Come Holy Spirit fill the hearts of thy faithful... I prayed.*) I put an arm around my son and we talked about how blessed we were to have such a grandma. Then I spoke gently and said there might be a problem with some of the toys; we would talk it over when Dad came home. Christopher, mature and in control but very vulnerable still wanted an explanation from me: "Christopher, what is the reason for Christmas?" Mystified he quickly answered that it is the birthday of Jesus. "So, if Jesus came to His birthday party, do you think He would want to play with Transformers?" A sense of dismay moved across his face as he realized the inevitable. A long heavy silence followed.

"Okay, Hannah, I'm coming," he shouted in reply to his sister's urgent beckoning to go outside. Before leaving the room Christopher turned to me with a knowing look that belied his years and gave me a hug. Now it was my turn to stand in disbelief.

Mary Dahl Maher

Two Sides to Every Story

Sunday morning I got a call from Steve, my eldest son, twenty years old, asking me to bring $500 to post a bond, as he had spent the night in jail and could not be released without bond. Now where on a Sunday morning do you get $500? (This was before ATMs.) Well that is what bondsmen do. My husband had had a chemo treatment on Friday and was still in no condition to drive. So I had to call the bondsman, go and get the money, and then go to the jail. I was worried and confused—this didn't seem like Steve.

As I pulled into the parking lot at the jail, a man got out of a car that had pulled in ahead of me. The man slammed the door as hard as he could and stormed up to the jail. I entered right behind him. We gave our names to the officer at the desk, who called to the officers in the cell block. Another young man came out first. The man in front of me was his father. He began cussing and swearing at his son. Hearing this calmed me down. When my son came through the door, I went up to him and hugged him and put my arm through his to walk outside.

Once we were in the car, I asked him how he had ended up in jail, and Steve told me the whole story. His best buddy John, the same age as Steve but married for a little over a year, had had a big argument with his wife and was really upset with her. That evening he asked Steve if he could borrow his car. Later when Steve went out to his car he found a large collection of tools in the back. Just then the police arrived and arrested Steve because the tools were stolen from a local contractor. Steve was taken to the county jail. By the time we got home there was a call from the man whose tools had been taken. He said John had returned the tools. Soon John returned Steve's car and said he was very sorry.

John and Steve remained good friends for many years. My son learned an important lesson that day: that no matter what, his family would always trust and support him. I learned one too: not to judge my children until I heard their side of the story.

Patricia Urban

"Trust is the nourishment of life."

—Isaac Bashevis Singer

Teaching Simplicity

Sometimes the values we try to teach backfire. I have one memory that stands out when life didn't go as planned. Our family has always enjoyed traveling. We especially valued the simplicity of camping and the chance it gave us to get away from the complications of everyday life. Camping was a time when our young family could enjoy nature, new surroundings and each other. Camping in Nova Scotia's Cape Breton provided just such an opportunity.

As we pitched our little tent where the six of us prepared to sleep, a park ranger drove up and warned us of an impending storm. We chose a more appealing fluffy-green spot away from the bare, rocky hill on the back side of our assigned camping area. With some encouragement and persuasion, our four little "rabbits" fell into deep sleep, soon followed by their travel-weary parents. Around 2 AM we awoke to the sound of thunder and movement under our sleeping bags! The tent floor was writhing like a water bed. Rainwater from the hill above us was gushing down onto our camping spot and under our tent. What to do?

My husband and I took turns carrying the girls to the car which in the torrent of rain seemed to be miles away. Fortunately before leaving for Canada, I had packed a new box of large garbage bags behind the front seat. We proceeded to fill the garbage bags with every drenched item in and around the sagging tent. Then at last we stuffed the tent and poles into the bags.

Try to picture this: steaming car windows, frustrated, exhausted parents, wet, cold, crying thumb-sucking children buried beneath big, black plastic bags and family dog Debbie shaking water all over us as we drove down the muddy rain-washed road. The picture was not pretty. The Holiday Inn was a beautiful sight that early morning. Behind the hotel there was a hill that faced the sun, well suited for drying out wet camping gear. We also found a light pole to tie up Debbie. The equipment dried, but the smell of "wet dog" lingered in the car. The hotel with all the luxuries of home saved us. So much for simplicity!

Patricia Costigan

TRADITIONS

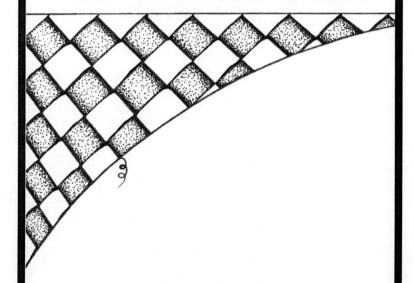

Celebrating Life Together

"Family traditions counter alienation and confusion. They help us define who we are; they provide something steady, reliable and safe in a confusing world."
—Susan Lieberman

———⊸⊗⊶———

5

Traditions

Celebrating Life Together

"But, Mom, you always put an ornament in my shoe on the Feast of St. Nicholas. Couldn't you have put one outside my apartment door?" My son was 19 and living in his own home when he made the request to continue our family tradition. Each child would receive an ornament and candy in the empty shoe they placed outside their bedroom door on the eve of the Feast of St. Nicholas. He loved the "surprise" and wanted to hold on to it, even into adulthood.

Meaningful traditions are part of the weft and the warp that weave a family together, giving it strength and structure. They make connections within the family and between generations, creating feelings of closeness and a sense of identity. Traditions create memories and then memories become an ongoing part of the tradition.

Carrying on traditions from earlier generations and establishing new ones for a family take thought, preparation and effort. They need not be complicated, just deliberate. I once read that Susanna Wesley, wife of Rev. John Wesley, Anglican cleric and Christian theologian, had 17 children. She set aside one hour a week to spend with each child! This inspired me to create "together time" with each of my five children. This could be as special as an overnight stay at a bed and breakfast just with Mom or as ordinary as a walk in the park. "Together time" sometimes brought me unexpected surprises. On one "together time" trip to the Children's Philharmonic, my shy, quiet middle child talked non-stop to and from the concert hall.

Traditions come in all sizes and shapes. They can be as common as a bedtime story, as memorable as a family trip, or as simple as making a practice of saying, "I love you." Traditions are formed as birthdays are celebrated, religious milestones are marked and as family members come together for holiday events. In these and all the varied moments of a shared life, from the simple to the profound, traditions strengthen and celebrate a family's life together.

Diane Knittle

The Big Day

It was bedtime and our oldest child was filled with excitement because the next day was her birthday. Catching her enthusiasm, my husband and I wanted to do something special and unintentionally began a birthday tradition for our young family.

We always ate at the kitchen table, and on the night before the "big day," after the birthday child went to bed, we hung colorful streamers from the ceiling. We decorated the birthday child's chair with crepe paper, finishing it off with a big bow. We made a sign with multi-colored markers announcing our daughters' or son's age. I made sure the table was set for breakfast with birthday decorations, placemats and cloth napkins. In the morning, the birthday child was the first one allowed into the kitchen. Even though the meal was standard breakfast fare, the birthday child started the day off feeling special. What I treasure most, though, is that as our children got older, they decorated the kitchen for my husband's and my birthdays.

I was eager to continue the tradition after our kids left for college. So when we went to visit our oldest for her birthday during her freshman year, we decorated the inside of the van. We hung streamers, created a birthday message on poster paper, and crafted a bow which we taped to the top of the seat. Eagerly, we escorted her to our van parked in the lot near her dorm. She became self conscious with our avid attention in this public place and, while she appreciated our effort, made it clear she was ready to leave this beloved tradition at home.

Sheila Roney

The Birthday Plate

When our children were young, our family was given a shiny red plate with white lettering that announced, "You are special today." This was always placed on the table in front of the birthday person. It instantly created a festive atmosphere and our children loved it.

Suzanne Shady

Birthday Eve Poem

On the night before each child's birthday, we recited this poem. Even now with those little children grown and living off in another state, we call and recite this verse. Amid giggles of embarrassment there is that same wash of deep joy, love and sense of being cherished.

The Birthday Eve Poem

When I have said my evening prayer,
And my clothes are folded on the chair,
And mother switches off the light,
I'll still be __ years old tonight.
But from the very break of day,
Before the children rise and play
Before the darkness turns to gold
Tomorrow, I'll be __ years old.
__ Kisses when I wake,
__ Candles on my cake! *

Suzanne Shady

* From *Festivals, Family and Food* by Diana Carey and Judy Large, Hawthorne Press, England, 1982

Birthday Bows

In our extended family, the birthday of a grandchild was always huge on the family calendar. First there was the party. Everybody would be running around playing party games, sitting, chatting, catching up on the family news and enjoying the festive moment. The crowd could number 8 or 28. It depended on the time of year and the people who were in town. A meal was always involved and gifts and cake and ice cream, of course. We had almost one party a month and sometimes more.

Over the years these parties took on a certain rhythm. They were not identical, changing in scope and menu depending on who the birthday child was and whose house we were at. But we knew what to expect and if things didn't happen according to schedule, the "special" boy or girl would invariably get everybody back on track, especially when it was time to open gifts.

There was a ritual that all the kids looked forward to birthday after birthday, year after year. When bows and ribbons were torn from the gifts, the birthday child would jump to his or her feet with great glee and stick the bow onto Granddad's forehead. For the duration of the gift opening, he would sit with a cheerful smile on his face as more and more bows were added. Of course he always looked silly but he never discouraged his precious grandchildren from this activity.

Then there came a year when Granddad was not there to play his part. The forehead decoration became a part of the past, living on only in memories that the

32-year-old cousin remembers as fondly as the 15-year-old. Surely this is as much a gift as anything that came wrapped with a glossy bow.

Jo Ann Figueiredo

Family Day

Sunday was family day. First, all ten of us would squeeze into the station wagon and go off to church together. On the way home we stopped for donuts. Everyone got to choose which kind they wanted. After devouring the donuts at home, everyone changed into play clothes appropriate for the day's outing.

During the summer, it was canoeing on Lake Ontario. We had one canoe, and though we often borrowed another, we still had to take turns. Eventually everyone learned how to paddle. Swimming in the lake and making sand castles in our friend's cove was also part of the day.

In the fall, Sundays were apple day. We found a grower down the road who let us pick the "drops," apples that fell to the ground. We owned an apple chopper and press and would invite another huge family to join us to make cider. There are a lot of steps in the process, so many hands made light work. After cleaning up we shared a meal. Of course, cider was the beverage and apple pie was the dessert.

When wintertime rolled around, we went cross country skiing, pulling a sled with the youngest on board, or ice skating on the frozen pond in the pasture near our home. The boys tapped maple trees in February and in March and we made maple syrup. We boiled the sap down over an outside fire between snowball fights and snow sculpturing.

During inclement weather, we all gathered around our large dining room table, with the two extra leaves put in, and worked together on big jigsaw puzzles. When someone got bored they wandered off to do their own thing, but always came back to help put in the last pieces. Popcorn and cider were good as snacks for puzzle making. Regardless of the weather or the season we always spent Sunday together.

Patricia Urban

A Tradition of Traditions

For over ten years, a tradition in the O'Toole household was traveling to one set of grandparents in Cleveland, Ohio, or the other in Ridgefield, New Jersey, for the holidays. As parents, we tried very hard to alternate the holidays so no one ever felt slighted. After having four children in nine years, things got interesting. The time between Thanksgiving and Christmas was simply insane. Gift shopping and wrapping, added to the usual laundry, cooking, and cleaning, was a challenge. At the time, who thought this was tradition?

In 1988, we landed in Walworth, NY. Our oldest child, Kimberly, was starting kindergarten and the promise of a permanent job for my husband was just too good to ignore. We continued with our holiday traveling tradition until she was in seventh grade. She wondered why our holiday destination was always changing. She was looking for a set tradition and wanted to spend time with her friends over school breaks.

Kimberly's best friend, Clare, lived close by and her extended family was also far away. Our similar situations pulled us together into a new extended family. For the last ten years, the two families have celebrated New Year's, St. Patrick's Day, and all the other holidays we can think of together. We share each other's deepest thoughts and prayers. We laugh and cry. We've had holidays with adults and children missing. We've sent our children to faraway places for travel and study. Sometimes it takes another family to help you find your own traditions.

Elizabeth O'Toole

Sharing Traditions: Creating Extended Family

Photos of our family's first Thanksgiving in Rochester, NY, reveal our four daughters with sad little faces above their lovely dresses and patent leather shoes. The pictures show how we tried to make it a special day with just us and how painfully lonely it was. That was the first time we celebrated Thanksgiving far from our loving extended family. We sorely missed celebrating holidays with our grand assortment of aunts, uncles, grandparents, and cousins.

When our oldest daughter, Clare, entered grade seven at a new school, she met her best friend. Kim O'Toole had three siblings the same ages as our other three daughters. Their family was also transplanted with no relatives to share special events. We began by celebrating Easter together. We continued with Thanksgiving and then with the parade that passes in front of our house each July 4th.

During these celebrations new traditions evolved. One Easter, Liz O'Toole began the presentation of the "bird cage" flower arrangement—a very large arrangement with twigs in the shape of a birdcage. This arrangement now appears at every gathering. Then there is the traditional carrying of the bench from our back yard to the driveway for the Fourth of July parade. Immediately upon arrival, Dad O'Toole and son, Tom, put the official bench in place for parade viewing. Only after all is set are hugs and greetings exchanged.

Through the years the two families have shared graduations, confirmations, travel stories, deaths, tears, laughter and life. We have become parents, grandparents, aunts, uncles and cousins for each other.

Patricia Costigan

Gifts from the Heart

The Sunday after Thanksgiving began our family "preparation" time for Christmas. Each child wrote their name on the same size and color of a piece of paper, folded it and put it in a basket. Then Mom and Dad would help each child draw a name—with eight children this was easier than with only two or three. The person whose name was drawn was the sibling for whom they would make a gift. Yes, make. This involved a lot of input and physical help from Mom and Dad. My oldest son loved fudge, so he was frequently the recipient of a large batch of fudge! If a child had a collection, an addition to it was always welcome. The girls frequently sewed with Mom's help: clothes for a sister's favorite doll, a stuffed animal for a baby sister or brother, a shirt for an older brother and so on. The boys tended to work with Dad on a carpenter project—a doll house, a toy box, a wooden train. As they got older and started to earn money from babysitting, yard work or picking fruit, they would purchase the gift. This practice continues today, even as they are spread across the country from California, to Washington State, New Hampshire, Massachusetts, New Jersey and Michigan.

Patricia Urban

Holding on to Hope

Advent calendars seemed to fill a void for my husband and me as we waited for the day of Jesus' birth during those many years of trying to conceive a child ourselves. Opening a tiny door, we read the Advent prayer, "Blessed is she who believed in what the Lord has promised" and continued to be hopeful. When our miracle babies came, we carried on the tradition. As a family, opening each little door and discovering the picture or verse hidden there captured each of our imaginations and focused us on the true meaning of the season.

Suzanne Shady

Game Night

Many Christmases ago, Nintendo was a greatly desired gift, which Santa brought to our three girls. Unfortunately, Santa had not consulted me. I did not want Nintendo for my children. I wanted them to continue reading books together, playing card games or board games like "Sorry," not playing video games. The rest of the family realized how sad I was at having Nintendo in the house and agreed, under a bit of pressure, that Santa could pass the gift on to someone else.

The story is still told today of how "deprived" my children were by that parental action. However, they now understand how right that decision was for our family. Now the three girls and their little brother can't wait to have game night to play "Family Feud," "Cranium," or Canasta. Game night has become a tradition when the grown siblings and spouses are together at Christmas or on vacation together.

Patricia Bertucci

Christmas at Home and Away

The details were taken care of—another Christmas Eve was upon us and all the children were home. Our children were no longer two to twelve or six to sixteen, but twenty-one to thirty-one, and they still wanted their stockings outside their door. On Christmas morning they still wanted the same foods for brunch: cinnamon rolls, egg strata, and orange blossoms—our favorite breakfast drink. They still needed a time that they could get out of bed and congregate, examine stockings and then come to our room squeeze onto the bed and share the items from their stockings. They needed their father to go light the tree as they sat squished together on the steps for a picture before descending to open presents.

Traditions comfort and unite. They soothe and are the making of memories. So when our oldest daughter, Sarah, was in Thailand one Christmas, it was reassuring for her and for us to know that she was carrying on some of the same traditions as we were back home. For us that's what makes Christmas, Christmas.

Patricia Bertucci

Recipe for Orange Blossoms

Yield 6 to 8 servings
1 6-ounce can frozen orange juice concentrate
1 cup milk
1 cup water
⅓ to ½ cup sugar
1 ¼ teaspoons vanilla
12 ice cubes
Sprigs of mint for garnish

1. Blend all ingredients together, except ice.
2. Add a few ice cubes at a time, beating at high speed until all crushed.
3. Garnish with a sprig of mint and serve immediately.

Twelfth Night

We always celebrated Twelfth Night in our family. The twelve days of Christmas end on January 6, which was the day the three kings came to worship the Christ Child. My husband made a wooden and cardboard camel with "net" saddle bags. This camel appeared around New Year's Day and moved a little closer to the manger scene under the Christmas tree every day. Slowly his saddle bags swelled with small packages. On January 6th the camel with saddle bags bulging arrived at the manger as did the figures of the three wise men!

After dinner that night the story of the three wise men was read aloud and the packages from the camel were opened. Then the party began! Guests started arriving around 7:30 PM. The driveway was lit with flaming torches made by the older boys, and eggnog, punch and munchies were set out.

After everyone arrived, we cut and served the Three Kings' Cake. Buried in the cake were three pennies. Whoever got a penny in their piece was a "King." A "Mary" and "Joseph" were chosen, and the Twelfth Night Mummery Play began. Every year my husband wrote a new script. Various people were assigned to "vocal effects" i.e. cold wind, rustling trees, etc. When everyone knew their role, a trumpet sounded from upstairs and gradually all descended followed by my husband in outlandish robes. "Hear ye, Hear ye, Hear ye" was the introduction to his Twelfth Night script.

The night always ended with the Bible story of Jesus' birth, and those guests chosen for Mary, Joseph and the "Kings" assembled in a tableau before the Christmas tree/ manger scene while all sang "Silent Night."

Patricia Urban

The Time Capsule

Each year as the holiday season approached, a group of friends would plan some special events. In the weeks before Christmas, our families went caroling in the neighborhood. We met to make gingerbread houses using graham crackers, frosting, and an assortment of candies. One family hosted an annual Christmas Eve open house.

New Year's Eve was planned just for grown-ups. This changed, however, as the children grew older and we parents realized that all too soon they would be off on their own celebrating with their friends. We took turns hosting this yearly event and our children waited with happy anticipation. Some years we played games such as charades, had a "White Elephant" exchange or partook in a scavenger hunt. Other years we ventured to a bowling alley, an ice-skating rink, went sledding, and watched the fireworks downtown. Of course food was always involved.

In 1999, excited about the millennium, we decided to create a "time capsule." By now some of our children were young adults living on their own, so four couples and a few of the younger children gathered to celebrate the coming year. During the evening, as we placed each memento in a sturdy box, we shared what the item meant to us. In went a cross, a Star of David, pictures, poems, a pair of Irish dance shoes and other items that represented faith, family and friends. One couple became the keepers of the capsule and when they moved from New York State to North Carolina the box went with them.

Now our children are scattered all over, from Hawaii to Virginia and places in between, celebrating New Year's Eve with their own new families or friends. And I know that when we decide to open our capsule sometime in the future, all the wonderful memories of our New Year's Eve tradition will come pouring out.

Sheila Roney

"In truth a family is what you make it. It is made strong... by the rituals you help family members create, by the memories you share, by the commitment of time, caring and love you show to one another, and by the hopes for the future you have as individuals and as a unit."
—Marge Kennedy

The Blessing of the House

Growing up in a small town in upstate New York, I have vivid memories of greeting each New Year at my grandparents' home with my parents and siblings and lots of aunts, uncles, and cousins. In an era when children were supposed to be quiet and well behaved, this night we were allowed to stay up late, eat exotic treats such as potato chips and French onion dip and creamy eggnog, and make the most noise possible.

As soon as the countdown to midnight began, we children would tumble out the front door into the cold air with noise makers ready to usher in the New Year. Wooden rolling pins, metal spatulas and aluminum pots were perfect for the occasion. The darkness of the dimly lit street added to the primeval desire to bang and hoot long and loud as we welcomed another year of hope and promise. Sometimes we would meet other neighbors engaging in the same ritual, and we would try to drown out one another. We'd clamor and carry on until my grandfather emerged onto the porch with a bottle of holy water.

There was instantaneous silence! It was time to listen respectfully as our patriarch called upon God to bless our house and all who would pass through its doors in the year to come. He sprinkled the water raising his mighty forearm and making the sign of the cross at the front of the house and again as we circled each of the four corners. Though I don't remember the exact words, I clearly remember the feeling of safety and connectedness in the knowledge that I belonged to an Irish Catholic family who, by the grace of God and the intercession of His mother, Mary, could overcome any obstacle placed in our path.

Mary Dahl Maher

God bless the corners of your house and
all the lintels blessed,
And bless the hearth and bless the board
and bless each place of rest,
And bless each door that opens wide
to strangers as to kin,
And bless the rooftop overhead
and every sturdy wall.
The peace of man, the peace of God,
with peace and love for all.

—Irish Christmas Blessing

The Easter Bunny

The Easter Bunny who came to our house was very imaginative. If the weather was cold or damp, the Easter baskets were hidden inside—anywhere—attic to basement, behind the piano, or hanging from the cellar beams. If the weather was nice, baskets could be in the barn, the garage, the garden house, or in a tree or bush.

Teenage Easter Bunnies were the most imaginative. One year they really got carried away. All baskets were hidden outside. The younger children and teens found their baskets fairly soon. Mom and Dad were then told the Easter bunny hid baskets for them too. Dad took only fifteen to twenty minutes to find his attached to grape vine wires.

That left only me to find my basket. I went through the house again, back to the basement, the laundry room, inside and outside the washing machine, dryer, beams, and boots. Then everyone trooped outside again with me in the lead listening to voices chiming, "getting warmer" or "colder" or "freezing."

As I walked around the house they began to chant "look high" or "look low." The "look high" chant was louder as we neared the front of the house. I could be a little dense some times, but when the "look low" chant was a whisper and the "look high" was a shout, I finally caught on. There it was—a large beautiful Easter basket midway between two second floor windows on the edge of the front porch roof. When I finally spotted it the cheers rose, hands clapped and I got nine high fives.

However, I still had to retrieve the basket. Running up to the boys' bedroom, I then climbed through the window which was open and held up the basket with melting chocolate bunnies for all to see.

Patricia Urban

Grape Pie Day

Our children were not thrilled with our idea; I think they called it "boring." New to upstate New York, Bill and I decided on an "old fashioned Sunday drive" to get a glimpse of our new surroundings. We set out on the road south of Rochester with Beth and Mike (then 11 and 9). As we drove, we saw a marvelous flock of grackles swarming in unison across the corn fields. We came upon beautiful, multi-colored hang-gliders sailing off of Bristol Mountain. Following signs for "grape pie" we caught a look at Canandaigua Lake as we headed toward Naples, NY. It is a quaint little town built around a winery.

Out of curiosity we followed the signs to "Cindy's Homemade Pies" and bought a grape pie straight from her kitchen. At a deli nearby we bought forks and went to a nearby park to try out this new culinary delight.   It was delicious. The adjoining overgrown cemetery was the perfect place to play hide-n-seek. Going home by another route we came upon an apple farm offering us a chance to take a wagon ride to "pick our own." What a perfect day, not so boring after all.

Our grape pie adventure turned into an annual event. As our family grew by three more children so did our "Grape Pie Day" and over the years we also included grandma, neighbors, relatives and friends. There were years we had one or more sulky teen grudgingly going along for the ride. Thankfully they are all adults now and after thirty "Grape Pie Days," they bring everyone they can to join the fun.

Diane Knittle

"Kids don't necessarily like them when they're young. But traditions mean everything when they're older."
—Irene Costigan, 18 years old

An Irish Blessing

May the road rise to meet you.
May the wind be always at your back.
May the sun shine warm upon your face,
the rains fall soft upon your fields
and, until we meet again,
May God hold you in the palm of his hand.

This simple Irish blessing has become a very important part of our family celebrations over the years. My dad chose it to toast family and friends at the weddings of his four children. He also used it to welcome and thank people who attended his own fiftieth wedding anniversary party. My brother used it to end the eulogy at my dad's funeral and once again stood with glass in hand to share it at his niece's wedding. My youngest daughter chose it to end her valedictory speech at her high school graduation, invoking it as a family tradition and making it a gift to all there. My brother-in-law used it as his oldest son got married. Two months later my husband brought us all together with a sweep of his arm as he recited the familiar words at his second daughter's wedding. My mom, Grammie to 16 grandchildren, is busy giving a framed copy to each one as they marry and settle into their own homes just as she did for her children many years ago. I'm sure it will be an important part of our family into the next generation and beyond.

Jo Ann Figueiredo

FAITH

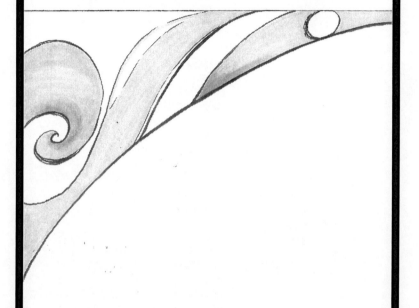

Strong Roots to
Nurture and Guide

6

———

6

Faith

Strong Roots to Nurture and Guide

There was a beautiful painting hanging in our living room as I was growing up: the Lone Cypress on Monterey Bay, California. It is a striking portrait of a majestic tree growing out of the rock. This image, which represented the view my father saw returning from WWII, held great meaning for him. It symbolized perseverance, strength, inspiration, and faith. For my parents that faith was the rock which sustained them through the harshest times and was also the source of joy and renewal. It is this rich legacy of faith that has guided my own spiritual journey.

"Faith" has many meanings: complete trust or confidence; a firm belief and trust in and loyalty to God; belief in the traditional doctrines of a religion. Whether we are religious or not, born into a faith tradition or searching for what we believe—we are on a journey. Our life experience, our unique story is critical to the process. Ultimately, we need to search, doubt, and question and make what we believe our own.

For the nine of us moms, faith in God is a legacy given to us by our parents. We can see the roots of our faith, seeds that were planted and nourished in our families through the generations. We recognize the incredible gift that it is and now we want to give it to our children. Our decisions to strive to make this faith our own, to believe without seeing and to make re-peated "leaps of faith" into the arms of a loving God, has given us the confidence to share these beliefs with our children. They in turn, by asking difficult questions concerning life and death and the nature of all things, have forced us to re-examine what we believe in, ma-turing our faith while nurturing theirs.

Raising children helps enormously in this task. Our children will ask all the 'Big Questions': "Who made those stars? Is Grandma in heaven now? Why did kit-ty have to get hit by a car?" And they expect us to answer them. They push us to think about and articu-late our beliefs. Children call us to be authentic and credible teachers—on the spot! It is a challenging and rewarding endeavor through which parent and child grow together.

While our children inspire our faith to grow, they are also likely to be the greatest test of our faith. Their mis-behaviors are singularly able to undo us. Our children in trouble pierce our hearts and their personal choices can evoke the deepest emotions. At such times, faith is like a tripod that maintains our balance: we need to have faith in ourselves, faith in our children and the upbringing we've given them and faith that God will bring us through it all.

None of us escape the difficult times in life. Children, also, will face tragedy or loss, and will confront negative pressures from peers and the modern culture. Those who are formed in faith are given resources that lend direction and comfort. However, the seed of faith planted by parents or grandparents, mentors or heroes must be tended to assure growth. Then, it will bear fruit that opens us to newness and possibility, the opportunity for transformation and self-discovery.

No matter our age, faith leads our hearts into a re-newing relationship with God that can sustain us and provide a deeper meaning for all that we do. This faith becomes the rock that is a steady foundation for our lives and theirs, which will nourish and guide us through the years.

Suzanne Shady

Faith Flows Downhill

When my Dad was alive, one of his favorite sayings was "Love flows downhill." By this he meant that when we love our children the love flows down to them. It may not be returned to us with gratitude in the moment but our love is in a constant flow down to the next generation and beyond. Faith can be described that way as well.

In his many stories, Dad spoke about how he was part of a German Catholic parish where he grew up. He explained experiences of adoration, Our Lady of Perpetual Help devotions, the rosary, Easter services, and Midnight Mass. He told those stories of church devotions but he lived the faith. He lived the strength of his conviction that there is a just God who always loves us.

I did not know my grandparents but I knew their faith through the strength in commitment and unwavering belief my parents had in Christ, the saints, and Our Lady. My parents clearly stated that their job was to help us get to heaven. They wanted to be in heaven with us some day along with Aunt Hilda, Uncle Oscar, Tanta Anna, and Grandma Gertrude.

The Church has changed since Dad and Mom were growing up in the early 1900s but their faith continues to flow downhill to future generations.

Patricia Costigan

Simple Faith

"Mommy, would you pray that I get better?" asked our seven-year-old daughter. It was the season of a particularly nasty flu. Beth had been vomiting during the night and into the morning. I laid hands on her and asked the Holy Spirit for her healing. Her little body was so exhausted from fever, dehydration, and lack of nourishment. To our dismay her condition showed no improvement. As I brought her a cold cloth for her forehead she asked, "If you prayed for me, why aren't I getting better?" I tried to answer the very difficult question. I said, "Well, sometimes more people who care about us have to be praying too."

Without a blink of an eye she requested, "Well, then call my friend Laura and ask her to pray for me!" Shortly after I talked to Laura and her mother, and was assured that they would pray for Beth immediately, her body responded to the prayer and she quieted down. Some may say it was just coincidence but you will never convince Beth of that. When she woke from a nap she said, "I get it, Mommy, we need the people who care about us to pray for us!"

Diane Knittle

"Prayer, like all good habits, is best learned while we are young."

—William Bennett

Tending the Seed of Faith

Faith, to my family as I was growing up, meant trusting in God, accepting His will, and following His commandments. It wasn't a sentiment but a practice, a way of living and structuring one's life. As a child, I attended Catholic schools. One of the religion lessons that was repeated throughout those years was "The Parable of the Sower" (Matthew 13:1-9). In this parable, Jesus tells what happens to seeds that were sown on different types of ground. Only the seeds that fell on good soil bore grain.

I knew there was good soil all around me in my family. My mother was a woman of great faith. She would tell me how when she was growing up in Ireland, her father would work all day in the fields of their small farm and after the evening meal get on his knees to lead his family in the rosary. The roots of her faith were strong and she continued to say those prayers daily throughout her life.

Even so, there were a few years in my young adult life when I did not attempt to nourish my faith. However, because of my parents' commitment, I was not allowed to neglect the faith tradition that had been given me. I continued to go to church on a weekly basis, and after awhile I experienced a desire to do more than just go to church and began to teach a religious education class. So even though the nourishment had been scant, the roots had remained strong.

My faith nurtured and guided me as I was raising my children. Every parent knows what a daunting task it is to raise a child. There are so many factors in our culture that intrude upon one's vision of what one's family will be like. There are choices to be made on a daily basis: age-appropriate clothing; television, internet and movie content; activities with friends; dealing with peer pressure. I was able to call upon my faith when decisions needed to be made and to say with conviction as countless mothers before me, "I don't care if everyone else is doing it, you're not!"

There is a saying attributed to Aristotle: If you want to be good, watch what the good person does, do likewise, and gradually you will become good. I think this applies to faith as well. I had the example of my parents and my older siblings and God's grace to help me tend the seed of faith I had been given. Now I have to have faith that my grown children will continue to develop their own relationship with God.

Sheila Roney

Teaching Religious Education

Our six children collectively taught 25 years of religious education for our Roman Catholic parish during their high school years. We felt that it was a way to give back to the parish family that had nurtured them over the years.

There was also a more practical reason that we embarked on this specific service. I noticed as my oldest daughter grew through middle school, she became increasingly more restless during Sunday mass and I thought that maybe if she was somehow invested in the life of the parish she would be more attentive. Her experience teaching was so successful that all the other children in the family were signed up as they entered high school.

As teachers, our teenagers had to be in their classrooms on time every Sunday morning at 9 AM and were responsible for lesson plans and for finding a substitute if they couldn't be there. They had to talk to parents about discipline issues and homework that wasn't handed in. They met with the Religious Education Coordinator and had to cover a specific curriculum. They taught the younger children—kindergarten, 1st and 2nd grades—and were able to use the information they had learned over the years in their various Catholic schools.

As they taught they seemed to develop a sense of responsibility for the students learning from them. They sat up straighter in church and paid attention. They recognized their students at mass, quietly acknowledging those around them.

In the end I felt that our children benefitted as much from this experience in the classroom as the students they taught. It was no longer enough for them to know what made them Catholic, they had to share it. And in that sharing they made the religion their own.

Jo Ann Figueiredo

"Tell me and I'll forget; show me and I may remember; involve me and I'll understand."

—Chinese Proverb

Strong Roots

It was about 4:30 AM when the phone woke Jon and me out of a sound sleep. My sister Ann was on the other end of the line and she was crying. "I'm in the hospital. The baby was born. We named him Joseph, but he only lived for a little while. Pat, the only way I am going to make it through this is because of my faith in God." I got off the phone and sobbed. Ann had had shingles early in her pregnancy and Joseph had been born prematurely and with deformities. Ann had been on bed rest for three months to try to save this little life but it had not worked.

I'm guessing that Ann's reliance on faith was partly due to the fact that the foundation of her faith was so strong. Our parents had always put God first. On Christmas morning we went to church before opening one gift. As children we might have thought that was unfair but we did understand that attending Mass was the most important way to celebrate Christ's birth. We went to Catholic schools from kindergarten through college. Grace was said before meals and I can still picture my parents kneeling beside their bed to pray. Even though we are now adults, my father still sends us literature connected to the church and our faith. Faith can grow as we grow if the importance of that faith is acknowledged and that faith is nourished.

Patricia Bertucci

Family Camp

As we pulled into the parking lot, the exuberant teenagers surrounded our car, cheering and clapping, "The new family is here!" Clare, our oldest daughter, was huddled under her seat in the back while our three younger girls were in shock, not knowing what to make of the situation. And so began our first experience with Family Camp; none of us knew at that moment that this one week would lead to a lifetime journey of faith for us.

Family Camp, a.k.a. Camp Koinonia, is a Catholic Camp for family and personal renewal. It is nestled in the rolling hills of the Italy Valley in Western New York. Each camp day begins with breakfast and morning prayer. Then we divide into age groups for the themed morning session. After lunch, families have the afternoon free for hikes to the falls, sports, crafts, games, store, swimming, and just hanging out with each other. The early evenings are filled with activities like creating funny skits around the bonfire or square dancing. Then just before bedtime, each family member shares his or her day in the form of "high point, low point, and the point closest to God." Later in the evening while the teens care for sleeping children, the adults head to the store for laughter, sharing and support.

The Catholic liturgy is the heart of Family Camp. During each mass, kids experience music, storytelling and family engagement in a unique and very personal way. Families have the opportunity to plan the daily evening mass which enables them to express their creativity and deepen their involvement in the prayer community.

As years pass, the problems that families struggle with change—Thursdays at family camp don't. "Reconciliation Day" is an opportunity for families to spend significant time with one another, mending hurts and misunderstandings. This much needed day was always difficult for our family. As we discussed those individual behaviors that were painful to other family members, the process of forgiveness was both trying and healing. Thursday was a day of miracles which culminated with family absolution and a Mass of Reconciliation.

The teens were role models for our children. Our daughters wanted to grow up and share faith just like the teen staff. As our girls grew, each one of them worked at the camp in some capacity, learning from others and sharing their faith.

By the end of that first week we had become a family of families, experiencing a small Christian community. We saw our children excited about shared prayer in word and song, we experienced the selfless giving of spirit-filled teens and interacted with families striving to live in hope and grace—all this inspired us to be better parents and individuals.

My husband and I still attend camp by working in the store. We can't let it go. It is part of our family history. We love seeing other families experience Family Camp the way ours did for 18 years. We hope that our children will one day bless their children with the opportunity to enjoy a little piece of heaven in Italy Valley, New York.

Patricia Costigan

"Children do not need perfect parents, simply good enough parents. To support our children in their spiritual formation, we simply need to be on the journey with them, learning and growing, willing to say "I'm sorry" and to seek God's transforming grace, love, and strength."
—Scottie May, Beth Posterski, Catherine Stonehouse, and Linda Cannell, *Children Matter*

Eight Beatitudes for Mothers

Blessed are mothers...
who did without for us, they will be rewarded.
Blessed are mothers...
who lost sleep when we were sick, they will find rest.
Blessed are the mothers ...
who taught us how to pray, they will share God's kingdom.
Blessed are mothers...
who comforted us, they shall be comforted.
Blessed are mothers...
who taught us right from wrong, they will know justice.
Blessed are mothers ...
who showed us a life of faith by example, they shall live
forever.
Blessed are mothers...
who shared with us the meaning of peace, they shall know
peace.
Blessed are mothers...
who taught us the importance of loving God and each other,
they shall see God.

Be Still and Trust in God

Secular culture makes it a challenge to raise children today. I found strength in my faith and could be calm and trust God by praying the Scriptures: *"Write down the vision clearly upon the tablets, so that one can read it readily. For the vision still has its time, presses on to fulfillment, and will not disappoint; if it delays, wait for it, it will surely come, it will not be late." (Habakkuk 2:2-3)*

Habakkuk's words inspired me to choose a Scripture for each member of my family on New Year's Eve. I have done this for many years. I have written them in a journal or on a calendar. I would daily pray those holy words, relying on the promises they contained: *"The word of the Lord will not return void." (Is. 55:9-11)*

Some of these Scripture prayers were heartfelt cries for guidance, others for protection and still others in praise. I can look back now that my children are all grown and see very real ways in which God nourished and protected them: *"Like a shepherd He feeds his flock; in His arms He gathers the lambs, carrying them in His bosom, and leading the ewes with care." (Is. 40:11)*

Isaiah's words could not help but quiet my worried soul.

Diane Knittle

The Blessing

Each morning as my children left for school I blessed their foreheads. I made the Sign of the Cross and wished them, "God be in your day and with your friends." When the youngest of the five children was eight years old, I began graduate school. The three youngest would race to the door and say, "Now it is our turn to bless you." And bless they did, more than they could know.

Diane Knittle

Making Faith Our Own

During difficult times, faith becomes more important and takes on new meaning. In the early years of
our marriage we were struggling with the inability to
have children. We were searching for answers medically
and theologically. On one occasion we made a retreat
at Madonna House, a religious community of men and
women in Ontario, Canada. It helped us find a new perspective and gave us hope.

Raised Catholic in the 1950s, faith was part of the
air we breathed but there was an unspoken rule that it
was a quiet and personal affair "between you and God."
Hence praying spontaneously out loud or together as
a couple was foreign to us. However, Vatican II and the
Catholic Charismatic Movement "shook" things up.
While on retreat we got some interesting advice on this
topic.

We met with Fr. Francis, a resident priest, at the end
of the week, asking, "How can we hold onto the richness
we have found? We want to continue to grow spiritually
and in our relationship." After hearing about our lives
his advice was clear and simple:

1. Would I consider working part time or in a less
stressful job, while Ray finished his doctorate, so that
there was more time and energy for 'contemplative
time' and for one another? Marriages needed to be nurtured too, he said.

2. If you are serious, find one or two couples whom you could meet with regularly to pray and share life's joys and struggles.

3. Each night before going to bed say a prayer together, a short spontaneous prayer or the Our Father. This is not easy to do, he said, because when you pray, there is a deep intimacy, an opening up of oneself to the other. His love and compassion underscored the main point: if we made God a priority in our lives the Lord would richly bless us in return.

This experience began our conversion to a deeper, richer life of faith, individually and as a couple. We made changes in our lives. We had to take what we'd been given by our parents, teachers, and pastors and make it our own. This time of waiting was the rich soil which gave the seed of faith already planted room to grow. And grow it did—faith became something we could rely on, helping us through the trials of infertility, times of marital stress, and life crises. Over time, we could comfortably bring it into our family life—to our dinner table, our celebrations and other aspects of our lives. Finally, when children came and the promises of belief were deeply realized, we could share our faith with them.

Suzanne Shady

"Prayer is the mortar that holds our house together."
—Saint Teresa of Avila

Breaking the Ice Jam

One Friday evening the kids were fed, bathed, and ready for bed. We were waiting for Dad to call, saying that he had arrived at Dulles Airport and would be home soon. It had been a long and tiring week, home alone with a 6- and 3-year-old. Ray's promising new job, which would require one or two nights away each week, quickly became three and then four nights every week. Finally, the phone rang! I picked up the receiver and heard my husband's voice, choked with emotion, "Sue, I'm so sorry, I missed the flight. The next plane doesn't get in until 11:00 PM."

The stress had been building for both of us and this event pushed us to the edge. I had been feeling increasing resentment over this arrangement; this was not my idea of raising a family, not to mention sustaining a marriage. And to be fair, Ray wasn't happy either as he missed us terribly.

Ray's re-entry into family life after his week away was always hard for both of us. That next morning was worse than usual. I had developed my routines with the kids and had found a resourcefulness and strength in being able to manage alone. Ray was being extra helpful and solicitous, and that irritated me. The cumulative stress of the last months had just worn us down physically and emotionally. The tension between us was palpable.

Finally, I blurted out, "If we're going to make it through the weekend, I think we need to pray!"

Ray readily agreed. Then I was the one who felt awkward and reluctant. As we sat down on the living room couch, Ray gently took my hand. Physical proximity helped and we said a simple spontaneous prayer. That led to a rush of feelings and we engaged in heartfelt conversation. Most importantly the "ice jam" was broken and it helped us get back on the right track. We were able to move forward and could enjoy the day and a half with our children before Monday came again.

Suzanne Shady

One more thing: a gentleman doesn't go through life on his own. You will need prayer in your life. You will need to ask the Lord to help you and the Holy Spirit to guide you. Without prayer, you're only half educated. You may be smart, but if you're not respectful and you don't take responsibility, you're not a full person. Don't be afraid to ask God's help.

—Tim Russert, *Big Russ and Me*

Our Faith was Sorely Tested

The early years of my marriage and family life seemed idyllic, though hectic. Dick was a Classics professor at a small liberal arts college in Rochester, New York. We lived 25 miles away on a small farm, raising eight children and managing an assortment of chickens, pigs and rabbits, with a big garden that helped feed us all. It was hard work but I loved having a big family and we spent many happy times together.

Faith was an important aspect of our lives. Both Dick and I had come from strong Catholic families where belief was important. Dick in particular helped make faith part of the fabric of our family life—writing Christmas plays, creating ingenious holiday decorations and leading processions and celebrations in keeping with the church season. He made faith come alive in creative and fun ways.

Life took a dramatic turn in 1976, when Dick was diagnosed with cancer at the age of 45. He had to leave his job and we cared for him at home. In those days before hospice, this was unusual. As always Dick witnessed to his faith, taking each child aside to say goodbye and reassure them that he would be well in heaven and watching over them.

Then suddenly, I was widowed and raising eight children, the youngest of whom was 10. I needed to go back to school to get my teacher's certificate so I could support them. Our faith was sorely tested.

Suzanne was 16 and a senior when her father died. She began getting into trouble at school and she resisted help from her counselor. I was filled with worry. On the morning after her 18th birthday, she came downstairs with suitcase in hand. I said, "Sue, what are you doing?" She replied, "Mom, don't you remember? I said when I turn eighteen I'm going to move out!"

Nothing prepares a mother for that statement and the trail of fears that follow behind it. I could do nothing else but turn to God. Faith is like a tripod—I had to have faith in myself and my mothering, faith in my child and the upbringing I'd given her, and faith in God, that He would bring us through it all.

Patricia Urban

We Can Do Anything with the Lord's Help

As it draws near to a year since my mother passed away, I find myself thinking of the things she often said. One lesson she taught me as a child has remained with me.

My mom was widowed when I was five and my brother was seven. For six and a half years after my father's death, it was just the three of us. As we grew older, my brother questioned why we were not like the other families in our neighborhood. Looking back, I realize that this had to be a trying experience for her. However, she took the opportunity to teach us, "This is what the Lord has given us, so we need to make the best of what we have. The three of us can do anything with the Lord's help."

When my children were small, the days seemed to last forever and I often thought back to that time and realized that my mother had to have incredible faith in order to speak those words. Her confidence was a model of perseverance for me. Later, during those times when I found my faith shaken, I would look to my mother and remember.

Elizabeth O'Toole

"My mother planted seeds of faith and watered them with love."

—Alice Gray

The Gift of Religion

"Why, Mom, why did you send us to Catholic schools?" My 25-year-old daughter Kate, slight in stature and olive skinned, a lovely echo of her paternal Portuguese-Indian grandmother with my Irish blue eyes, looked intently at me as I started to explain.

Both my husband and I are "cradle Catholics." I for one never questioned this "inheritance" of belief. It was who we were and defined how we did things in my family. My husband's experience with his family was very much the same as mine; we were both educated from kindergarten through college in Catholic schools.

I didn't fully realize until I had children of my own that we had not inherited our religion like the color of our eyes or our complexion. Rather, some purposeful work must have gone into making it our own. This became clear to me after I had decided to put first our oldest child, Sara and then Kate, into the local public school.

As the days went on and I dutifully took my little ones to their Religious Education classes, an hour each Sunday morning, I became uneasy. I felt that there had to be more that we could do to help us reinforce our faith in addition to going to Mass on Sunday, learning bible stories, and saying prayers at home each night. I knew we needed help showing them the fullness of our religion and I realized that the right thing for us to do was to give them the gift our parents had given to us.

At about that time we moved to a new house in a new town and I enrolled them in the nearest Catholic school. Ideally I hoped to imbue in them the same sense of respect and reverence for God that I saw in their dad every day. But being more pragmatic I felt that if we kept them in Catholic schools for as long as we could, when they were grown and gone, they would certainly understand us and our reason for worshipping as we did. Then, if at some point they chose a different path, at least I would know that I had done my job and that whatever they decided to do, it would be with the full knowledge of their Catholic heritage.

Kate expressed some surprise at my answer. I think she just wanted to know why we were so willing to pay all that tuition. For us it was never about money, but about that gift of religion so seamlessly given that it appeared to have been a part of her and her siblings all along.

Jo Ann Figueiredo

"It dawned on me only slowly when I first had children that I held major responsibility for forming them in faith."
—*Bonnie Miller-McLemore*

Mother's Intuition

It was a late September afternoon and I was visiting with a friend at the home she had recently purchased. My three-month-old son was asleep in my arms and my two-year-old daughter was playing with my friend's four and a half year old. This little girl wanted to take my daughter upstairs to her playroom and my friend said that would be fine. She went on to explain that they had fixed up a room for her daughter to play in and it contained toys and a puppet theater, things a child would love.

As we chatted in her kitchen, I experienced a subtle feeling of unease about my two year old. I needed to see where she was playing. I was incredulous when I learned that the playroom was in the attic. As we walked up the stairway, I saw the attic floor was all around us; there was no railing at the edge where the floor opened to the stairwell. My heart stopped as I thought of the danger, knowing how a two year old can run with excitement and without thought of peril.

I made sure she was near me for the rest of our time and left for home earlier than I had planned. I was upset with myself for not having seen the playroom before the girls left. I felt weak when I thought of what might have happened. And I was grateful, so very grateful that I had listened to that intuitive feeling of impending danger to my child. I have always felt it was her Guardian Angel that kept her safe, alerted me to the risk, and urged me to act on it.

Sheila Roney

Wedding Faith

Three daughters—what a gift from God! The girls went to Sunday school or mass with us each week. They attended Catholic schools and sang in the church choir. When they were little, I sewed First Communion, Confirmation, and Christmas dresses. As they got older, I envisioned sewing wedding and bridesmaid dresses, if they wished. I pictured my daughters walking down the aisle of our church as they prepared to speak their vows in front of God, families, and friends. How different reality can be from dreams.

Our oldest daughter's wedding took place at a YMCA camp. The setting on a lovely lake was idyllic but clearly not what I had envisioned. The weather drove the ceremony inside, so we gathered in the camp's dining room to witness Sarah and Jason pledge their love for each other.

I had been raised a Catholic and embraced my faith. My daughter's spiritual journey had taken her on a different path and that was painful for me at times. Sarah had spent time in Nepal and embraced some of the peaceful meditative aspects of eastern religions. She was given a traditional red Nepalese wedding shawl and wore it at the beginning of her wedding. During the preparation time, Sarah's godmother expressed her concern to me and to Sarah that there would not be a Catholic priest at the ceremony. Jason was Jewish and there would not be a Jewish rabbi either. However, they created a very prayerful, spiritual wedding ceremony.

Sarah's godmother hugged me after the wedding ceremony and with tears in her eyes said, "I felt God's presence."

Both Sarah and Jason are aware of how much my faith means to me, of how much prayer and nurturing my spiritual side is vital to my existence. Jason has spoken of the prayer corner in their bedroom. They honor me as a faith-filled person through their expression of faith, just in a different way than I had imagined some thirty years ago.

Patricia Bertucci

CREATIVITY AND HUMOR

Keeping Life
in Balance

7

"Wear your life like a loose-fitting garment."
—Proverb

⸻

7

Humor and Creativity

Keeping Life in Balance

Hmmmm...a loose-fitting garment. Is that a flowing garment? Loose, flowing, go with the flow? Loose is the opposite of tight. Wearing life like a tight fitting garment sounds uncomfortable to me and to everyone around me. Loose sounds fun. Loose sounds like it has room for the creative ideas of everyone around. Even if their ideas are not so creative, loose includes those ideas and thoughts, too. It includes the acceptance of others and their suggestions and views. This favorite quote captures my artistic imagination. It reminds me to take myself and life lightly—to laugh, to be creative and sometimes to be a little outrageous.

Creativity is defined as the power or ability to invent. To bring into existence what was not there before. Creativity is not just for artists. Creativity is much broader and is required in many areas of life. Creative thinking is problem solving. No matter what we do we need the ability to be creative, to find new and better ways of doing things.

Humor is the ability to appreciate the comical, the absurdly incongruous elements of life. Humor refocuses reality and puts it in a softer light; it changes our perspective. For me humor is often born out of desperation at times when hurts sting. We found this to be true when my sister and I had the painful task of going through our mother's clothes after she had died. Our artist mom wore a favorite smock with oil paint plastered all over it. We discovered it had the ability to stand on its own when placed on the floor. Our howls of laughter and remembrance broke the somber mood with this moment of humor at a very sad time.

The wild cards of humor and creativity contribute to the Ha-Ha-Ha's and Ah-Ha's of family life. Humor and laughter are partners and two of life's important ingredients. The ability to laugh is cleansing, relieving and bonding. During unexpected moments of family frustration, pain, anger or embarrassment, humor can flip things inside-out if we are willing and able to take advantage of it. Staying open to humor, spontaneity and creativity helps us establish a loving environment and maintain balance in the lives of our families.

The memories we include here of funny family moments and stories of kid-inspired creativity provided our moms group with many opportunities for laughter as we met to bring this book to life. We particularly enjoyed sharing these stories because in the telling, we gave ourselves a chance to recapture for a moment the zest of our own young families' lives. We marveled at the memories and journals that have kept such vignettes funny, fresh and clear even after so many years. We now encourage you to be alert for these winsome moments as your family grows and suggest that you don't hesitate to take notes.

Patricia Costigan

The Prize-winning Sweater

I admit it, I love all of my clothes, but my many Christmas sweaters hold a special place in my heart. So when my middle daughter asked to borrow one of my special sweaters for a party, I was thrilled. She was delighted to be asked to attend and I wanted to make sure she enjoyed it, so the afternoon of the party, we went through my closet to decide which sweater would be best.

At the end of the party, when I went to pick up my daughter and a few of her friends for the ride home, I noticed that Colleen was quiet while the other girls wouldn't stop talking. One of them commented that Colleen had won the prize and what great fun the party had been. She was still quiet as the girls continued to chat among themselves as I dropped each off.

Finally Colleen and I were alone and I asked about the prize. Rather sheepishly, Colleen admitted that the contest had been for the ugliest Christmas sweater and she'd won first prize! So fearful that I would be upset, she could barely look at me. All I could do was laugh, loud and long. After a few moments, her worries melted away and we laughed together.

Elizabeth O'Toole

"… (a) sense of humor…is needed armor. Joy in one's heart and some laughter on one's lips is a sign that the person down deep has a pretty good grasp of life."
—Hugh Sidey

Holiday Crafts

For over fifteen years the centerpiece for our Christmas dinner table has been a wooden tree made of eight green graduated star shapes. They are piled on a wooden dowel and then one star, painted yellow, sits on its side on the top. What memories that tree brings back! It's the product of the years when our children made Christmas and Hanukkah gifts with five other families.

Put together six fathers, six mothers, fifteen to twenty children ages two to sixteen, paint brushes, fabric, sewing machines, thread, flour, sugar, eggs, beads and felt, macaroni and cheese, corn bread, brownies and four homes on a Sunday afternoon. What do you have? You have all the ingredients for a few hours of fun making Christmas and Hanukkah gifts.

For years a Sunday afternoon in November was designated for gift making for our six families. Imagine planning crafts for twenty children, 2 to 16 years old. We moms planned the crafts and got help from the dads to execute those plans. One year about 80 star shapes were cut from wood by a couple of the dads. The older children sanded, painted and then stacked them on a dowel to make Christmas trees and blue Hanukkah candle sticks. Another year, we cut fabric to sew fifteen aprons. Then there were the cookie years, the assembling wooden toy years…

Moms organized groups of children by ages and divided the tasks among three homes that were within walking distance of each other. Adults' talents were matched to the task at hand—painting, sewing, baking—all done with loving hands and patient words. Adults also escorted the younger groups of children between homes at designated times. Children's laughter resounded as they finished a gift and admired it. Then they hopped, skipped, and jumped to the next house. The children loved creating gifts and also loved the travel from house to house. After all the crafting was finished, we had a pot-luck supper at a fourth home.

The parents of these families still get together regularly and include the many adult children when they are in town. Memories of those fun times help us all reflect on the talents of the group and the individuals involved.

Patricia Bertucci

Dreaming

During those days when our children had some free time from school: summer vacation, weekends, holidays, the inevitable statement was made, "I'm bored." The responses were generally two:

1. "I have lots of things for you to do. Here, let's play the game…Choose a Chore."

2. With excitement in my voice: "How lucky you are. You can watch the pictures in the clouds, feel the rain, smell a tree, see the beautiful colors everywhere, look at the grass and watch the little ants and bugs scurry around the earth in search of food… This is your lucky day!"

One day after giving the latter response, I noticed my youngest daughter, Irene, outside squatting on the ground with her fingers in the grass, gently pulling away the blades, discovering the hidden mysteries below. Downtime is a precious time for imagination, creativity, discovery, and DREAMING.

Patricia Costigan

"The creative is the place where no one else has ever been. You have to leave the city of your comfort and go into the wilderness of your intuition. What you'll discover will be wonderful. What you'll discover is yourself."

—Alan Alda

Musical Duet

My sister Maureen and I seemed like opposites in every way. She was two years younger, shy, sweet, and sensitive to my bold, sassy, and tomboyish ways. Needless to say we were often at odds. In high school when we had kitchen clean up duty, we used to fight over the radio station. I wanted classical to accompany my duties, Maureen opted for rock, whether she was washing or drying. We'd flip the stations back and forth, but the dish drier always had the advantage of being closer to the radio. We were equally stubborn.

In this case we should have blamed our father. One of my earliest memories was when Dad proudly sat us down when we were ages 4 and 2 to listen to two musical records on our children's 45 rpm record player set up on the dining room floor. The first was "Daddy's Little Girl" and the other was "The Teddy Bears' Picnic." He sang them both to us with warmth and affection: "If you go down to the woods today, you're sure of a big surprise… Today's the day the teddy bears have their picnic." He invited us to imagine the scene and with great drama and play-acting he sang along with the music.

Later, when I was twelve or thirteen, he played a classical piece, Debussy's "The Afternoon of a Faun" and again created the imaginary scene. He had me try to listen carefully and "hear when the faun appears" in the music. It was a simple but magical moment that we shared together. Perhaps it was so meaningful because my dad's undivided attention didn't happen that often.

Besides leaving lasting and warm memories, these occasional and fleeting incidents planted a love of music in me that complemented my growing love for dance and drama. This combination led me to pursue multiple creative directions: from dancing in every school musical, to joining a dance troupe, to whirling and twirling my kids from the time they were babies up to adulthood. I have tried to pass on this wonderful legacy from my dad to my own children—I think successfully—for they too love music.

Recently upon hearing the melody of "The Teddy Bears' Picnic," a smile came to my face and I was transported to the day that my dad and his music helped me to feel that I was someone special.

Suzanne Shady

"If music be the food of love, play on."
—William Shakespeare

A Mother's Love is Stronger than an Alligator

It wasn't easy keeping three little ones occupied while grocery shopping. Peter, 5, was hanging on the outside of the cart, Mary Clare, 3, was in the basket. Paul, the 1-year-old, was in the cart seat.

Hoping to keep them contained I began telling them a story that I had just read in a magazine. I embellished it with many details to stretch the story out:

A new development was being built around an existing pond in a Florida area. Unknown to the developer and new residents was that a large, old alligator had his home at the head of the pond. Two young children played in the shallow water while the mother gardened. The old alligator slid quietly through the water toward the children. Just as the little girl spotted it and ran for the shore, the alligator took hold of the foot of her brother. When she screamed their mother came running. Without a thought for her own safety she ran into the water, grabbed hold of her son with one hand and started hitting the snout of the alligator with her other fist. A struggle ensued but with one particularly hard slug from the mother, the alligator opened its jaws. She pulled her little boy to safety.

The story captivated my children through the produce and meat departments. I finished in the middle of the cereal aisle. Suddenly, a woman pushed her cart up next to ours and said, "I was finished shopping awhile ago but I wanted to hear the end of the story!"

Diane Knittle

Child's Play

"Mommy, you funny!" my three-year-old exclaimed with delight. We were in the cozy bedroom she shared with her older sister and I was being silly. As I was folding her blanket-sleeper, I had slipped my hand into one of the legs of the sleeper and down into the foot. By bringing my fingers and thumb together, the foot folded into something roughly resembling a puppet head. This character then proceeded to say and do nonsensical things. My youngest child chortled with laughter as she enjoyed the magical transformation of her pajamas.

Sometimes creative moments happen upon us in simple unexpected ways as with the extemporaneous puppet; other times this creativity flows from child's play. I fondly remember my children playing that they were camping in our dining room. Customarily, the blanket draped over the dining table was the tent. They improvised a camping grill out of the heat register where they placed their toy pans and play food to cook a tasty meal to be shared by Mom, Dad, and whoever else happened to be around. The stairs to the second floor were a mountain to be scaled, often with great difficulty and accompanied by huffs and gasps as they approached the landing, happily on their way to the summit.

Sheila Roney

"Happiness is not in the mere possession of money: it lies in the joy of achievement, in the thrill of creative effort."
—Franklin D. Roosevelt

Kitty

Sara and Kate were close friends as well as sisters. They were a little more than a year apart in age and neither could remember life without the other. They were also my buddies as the younger children came along. We talked a lot about everything. One day baby Joe was down for a nap and Sara and Kate were just hanging around after lunch, doing whatever 2 and 3 year olds do before their naps. I had been thinking of changing Kate's nickname for some time. It seemed that the year Kathleen was born, every second baby girl was called Katie or Kate and I wanted to maybe mix it up a little. So half in jest I suggested that we might start calling her Kitty. Sara immediately looked up and said, "Great, then can I be Doggie?" And that is why Kate is Kate to this very day.

Jo Ann Figueiredo

Conesus Lake Olympics

One summer while we were vacationing with two other families at a cottage on Conesus Lake we watched the Summer Olympics on television. One mom suggested that our collective eight children, four girls and four boys, have their own Conesus Lake Olympics. The kids were thrilled with the idea and with the six parents as judges, competitions took place during the rest of the week. There were swimming races, rowing races, water skiing, soccer kicks, badminton matches, and fish catching just to name a few. The competitions were of a short duration since there were only eight participants and the age span of eight years meant that many of the activities were group events to help balance the varying abilities. This left both children and parents with plenty of free time.

Once started, the creative juices flowed. Colorful beach towels became the flags of the opening ceremony which each child carried. They followed one of the dads, who was carrying the torch to light the Olympic flame, a simple grill filled with charcoal that was sprinkled with lighter fluid.

The moms crafted Reese's gold-papered candies, York Peppermint Patties and Rollos into gold, silver, and bronze awards for the young competitors. And the children decided to prepare entertainment for the closing ceremony which took place our last night at the cottage.

Our Olympics became an annual event as our yearly vacation at the lake inspired the children to test their limits and go for the gold.

Sheila Roney

Legacy

When I was a child, my mother gave me one of the greatest gifts—the gift of sight. Whenever we went out, even just to the back yard, she would point out a sparkling drop of water on a flower, the color of the light before sunset, the shape of the shadow of a tree fallen on the ground. She taught me the appreciation of beauty. My mother is gone now but her gift lives on in me and in my children.

Patricia Costigan

Diamonds are a Girl's Best Friend

Shortly after we made the move from Reston, Virginia, to Princeton, New Jersey, I was at home alone with my rambunctious toddler, Raymond. Ordinarily a very happy and vivacious child, young Ray expressed his reaction to the turmoil of the move in his own unique way.

On this cold, February morning, as I peeled off his PJ's and wet diaper, he pulled away and went tearing through the house, glorying in his naked splendor. I found him in the living room, sitting on the sofa, with a sheepish look. This was the newly purchased sofa, our first brand new piece of furniture in 15 years of marriage. He was sitting in a large puddle that was slowly moving over and down the scotch-guarded cushions onto the cotton liner below.

I was by turns, frantic, furious, and then completely undone. I did not respond to my sweet little boy as a model mom—so then I spiraled down into the "failed mother" doldrums.

Raymond was nearly three and I wondering when I would EVER get him toilet trained. His older sister had been so easy. I had been told children will do it when they're ready but this was too much. I decided to try again with new vigor. Raymond's efforts so far were to sit on the potty chair, read a book, talk to me, and generally enjoy himself—with no results. I was exasperated.

So on this sunny winter day, as Raymond sat on his chair, the low hanging winter sun streamed in on us. It caught my diamond ring and I saw a bright, tiny ball of light reflected on the wall. I said, "Oh Ray, do you see what I see?" I jiggled the ring and the sparkle danced; he was enthralled. Slowly, I moved it over the wall and then down onto his chest and tummy. I said, "It's the tickle fairy and she's coming to get you. Here she comes..... closer......closer..." My little guy melted into gales of giggles. It was a moment of absolute delight. All of a sudden, he relaxed so much that a loud tinkle resounded in the pot. He was as surprised as I. Then came a whoop from me and a beaming smile for Raymond. We found the secret of success, and within a week he was toilet trained.

I learned from this experience that inspiration often comes to us in moments of motherly desperation. A friend of mine often said, when faced with a challenging situation, "Don't panic—it's all organic!" Meaning, the solution generally presents itself once you begin the task. We just have to trust ourselves and the process.

Suzanne Shady

"The world is but a canvas to the imagination."
—Henry David Thoreau

Emily's First Halloween

It was October 1986 and Halloween was upon us. Sara, Kate, and Joe were all veteran pranksters who already had two or three such holidays under their belts. I frankly don't remember their costumes. They might have been three blind mice that year, or a tramp, Mr. Man, and an alien from Halloweenland. But the highlight of my evening was Emily, my one year old. She was dressed as a snowflake. I had dressed her in white tights, white turtle neck, white sweater, and a white hat with ear flaps tied under the chin. I had covered her face with white costume makeup. She was darling and as I carried her from door to door, she got rave reviews which I accepted modestly. At every opportunity I told any interested candy givers just what she was.

As the evening was winding down, we got to the last street and a homeowner asked 'the question'. So, I turned and asked little Emily what she was, not knowing if she was even going to speak. She looked directly at the person asking the question and said, "Cornflake!" She certainly brought me back to earth when I realized she had no idea what she had been all along.

Jo Ann Figueiredo

Hannibal, the Rooster

We lived in Drayton Plains, Michigan with our children, only seven of them at the time. Dick felt it was time to teach at the college level and accepted a job at St. John Fisher College in Rochester, New York. It was a big move with seven children. Noel had finished first grade. Noel's class had incubated chicken eggs that spring and Noel was one of the lucky ones to get a new chick when they hatched. We had fenced in our yard so "Hannibal," the rooster, could strut all he wanted and nibble on plants in the garden, too.

We moved in early August. The household furniture was moved by van. Then all nine of us piled into the station wagon with our tent, change of clothes, and ice chest put on top. Hannibal, in his cage, was put on top of the car also. Everything was covered with canvas. Hannibal was not happy and every time we stopped he would crow!

We drove through Canada as it was shorter and faster. We did not know until we came to the border crossing that it was illegal to transport fowl without putting them in quarantine to check for diseases. Oops! We chose to trust our luck. The border guard stopped us, asked the usual questions, "Where are you going? Why? How long will you be in Canada? What is on top of the car?" We didn't mention the rooster, just said clothes, food, tents, etc. Then we heard Hannibal start to scratch and the older children burst into song. The border guard laughed at the kids singing and waved us through.

Crossing back into the United States at Buffalo, we told the children to sing when the border guard came. He just smiled and waved us through. When we arrived at our farmhouse and let Hannibal out, he was dizzy and couldn't walk in a straight line. He recovered in less than a day and became our "guard rooster." When the two youngest were outside playing, Hannibal would keep them from walking down the driveway past the house, and he wouldn't let them go under the fence into the pasture behind us where the horses were kept.

Patricia Urban

Digging to China

Beth, my college-age daughter wrote this story, remembering a potentially humiliating situation which was avoided by blending paint and humor. I chuckled the day it happened and she chuckled years later.

My small, chubby hands dig, flinging a dog-like spray of sand out from between bent knees. I love the way the grimy sand feels between my fingers, and imbeds itself below my fingernails. I want to dig to China. I would be the first out of all my sisters to do that.

On this particular summer day, the sky had the usual thick Rochester haze over it, the weather muggy. I was digging in the sandbox at the neighborhood park as usual, continuing the hole I had been tunneling for the past three days. I had peaked on Day Two, when I hit damp, dark earth. Now I was frustrated and tired, seeing I was not even an arm's length into the dirt. It was getting hot, and I was just about ready for a break. I stopped suddenly, taken aback. I had hit jackpot! My small fingers wrapped tightly around a dirt encrusted quarter so that no one could see my treasure. My three sisters were similarly digging holes nearby, and who knew what they would do for this. I was a wealthy woman, which worried me. Who could I trust with my secret? My mom would probably want me to give it to charity, and my sisters would unrelentingly pull my hair and slap my bottom until I gave up my newfound affluence. My dad would assure me that it would be invaluable "college money" and compel me to entrust it to the bank where I would surely never see it again.

I wanted to spend this money. I wandered into the park bathroom and sat next to the trash can to think. It always smelled like babies and old wax, but I felt this was where I could best think under the circumstances. I looked up as a young mother entered, pushing a stroller heavily laden with baby powder and diapers. There was a metal box above me. My answer! Right in front of my six year old eyes! The rectangular box had always held massive mystery to my sisters and me. But no longer. The sand had generously donated the 25 cents that would give me power over my sisters and would inescapably let me reign over the entire playground. No one else had this kind of money. Yes, this was my day.

I waited until the mother scurried away from my greedy eyes with her dirty baby diapers, to slide the freshly polished quarter into the waiting slot. I twisted the rusty handle with little difficulty. Down into my palm fell a cylindrical paper object. This odd tool was what I wasted my riches on? I felt tears welling up in my eyes, and scolded myself. My mom always told me that the impulsiveness would be my ultimate downfall, and so it was.

I ran home crying, jumping into my mother's waiting arms. She soothed me while I hiccupped my way through telling my loss. Mom laughed and gave me a big hug. "Bethy," she said, "How did you become so lucky to find such a treasure?" She told me it was a special paintbrush, one that she rarely used and only for special occasions. I looked up at her smiling eyes, with hope. I always wanted to be a beautiful artist like her. Now I could have my own supplies.

I sat down at the kitchen table in relief, while my mom brought me paint, and her special thick artist paper. Wondering why she only brought me different shades of red paint, I painted the afternoon away with her, marveling at the different textures and patterns that my special stick made.

Patricia Costigan

"All children are artists. The problem is how to remain an artist once he grows up."

—Pablo Picasso

Tickle My Funny Bone

I have these memories stored in my journals. Now and then I share these stories with my adult children. They love to hear how clever and funny they were when young and how they touched my funny bone:

- Michael, 4, and Beth, 6, often watched the students walking by our house on their way to the nearby high school. Beth, while eating one day at a fast food restaurant picked up a long, thin French fry and said to Michael, "Look! An Arthur!" Both giggled. The French fry reminded them of a tall, thin boy named Arthur who passed our house on his way to school. Forever after when someone in the family spots something or someone that is long and thin, we of course say, "Look! An Arthur!"

- Four-year-old Paul spotted blooming crocuses in March. "Look Mommy, the first flowers. They are ladies." "What would make you think that," I asked? "Simple," he said, "Ladies first."

- Two-year-old sister and three-year-old brother were side-by-side in their car seats when we happened to drive by a lovely farm where cows were grazing. Little sister removed her thumb from her mouth and exclaimed to her brother, "Look, Pete, pigs!"

- The first day of Little League was always a thrill for our "first game" players. The youngest of our three boys was eager to follow in his brothers' footsteps. He was sent out to the shortstop position in his new white pants and white uniform shirt. He immediately stooped down, filled his hands with dirt and initiated the new uniform from top to bottom so as to appear that he had "slid into home!" The fans in the stands rocked with laughter!

Diane Knittle

"The miracle of ordinary things fills children's worlds."
—William Wordsworth

Ruth Mary

Cherubic is the description that comes most easily to mind when describing the beauty of 5-year-old Ruth Mary. Her sparkling green-blue eyes and rosebud mouth were perfectly placed in a round little face topped with honey-brown ringlets. Ruth's innocent appearance belied the strong-willed, independent, and creative personality within. We can look back, now, and laugh at the summer she refused to take a bath. However, at the time, we were horrified at how incapable we seemed to be as parents in directing the behavior of our fifth child. In the end, we gave her a bottle of baby shampoo to play with in the inflatable backyard pool in hopes that she would accomplish the task of bathing herself.

When it was time for kindergarten, we looked for an environment where Ruth would develop the great potential we saw and decided to try the small classroom size of a suburban private school where one of her older brothers was a student. For all her demonstrative behavior, she was very shy when first meeting others until she could read the lay of the land. On assessment day, she chose a pretty floral skirt with matching sandals; she was born with innate fashion flair. She clung closely to my side as we were introduced to the teacher who had a very kind and gentle manner. Ms. Brown was understandingly patient when Ruth insisted on my staying with her.

She asked Ruth if she would like to draw a picture of herself. This is a standard test used to measure how children see themselves, and the detail in the picture reflects developmental age. The hope is that your little shining star knows she has a face with two eyes, a nose and mouth, and a body with two arms and two legs. Once Ruth was finished with her masterpiece, the teacher looked a little confused. In her unique way, Ruth had challenged the standard measurements, because she drew herself in profile so she had only one eye and one ear, but she had drawn long eyelashes and earrings, as well as nail polish on her very carefully rendered hands—no stick figure for her self-image.

I don't recall all the other questions, but when it came to the analogies test, there was another surprise waiting. Living in the city, Ruth had not seen many farm animals. Ms. Brown began by instructing Ruth to complete the sentence, "Cows give us milk and hens give us_____." My daughter squirmed into my side uncomfortably, and the astute teacher read this nonverbal language and tried another approach. Smiling she said, "Cows give us milk and chickens give us____." At the recognition that "hens" was another way to say "chickens," embarrassed Ruth hid her face in my skirt. Continuing in the same even tone, Ms. Brown repeated, "Cows give us milk and chickens give us eggs." Not missing a beat, Ruth replied, "and so do alligators!"

This is the gift of my independent child. She challenges me to grow in most uncomfortable ways but can also remind me how to laugh at the most ordinary things.

Mary Dahl Maher

"Common sense and a sense of humor are the same thing, moving at different speeds. A sense of humor is just common sense, dancing."

—William James

An Illuminating Adventure

Camping in Michigan proved to be an illuminating experience. We had to catch a ferry at 6:30 AM. We had left our house before sunrise and stopped for a potty break and exercise. The park we stopped at was a nature preserve and an outhouse was all that was available. We took turns, as it was a one-holer. The sky was still dark and there were no windows in the outhouse, so we passed the flashlight to the next person in line when we each came out.

My oldest daughter, 6, was the last to go in. She laid the flashlight on the seat beside her and when she stood up and pulled up her pants, it rolled into the hole. She came running out in tears and told us what happened. We all turned and looked at the outhouse glowing from the ground up. "It looks like it's radioactive!" said one of the older children. We piled into the car and laughed all the way out of the parking area and down the highway. We were wondering what the next visitors would think when they saw the "glowing" outhouse.

Patricia Urban

"A sense of humor is a major defense against minor troubles."

—Mignon McLaughlin

Wisdom

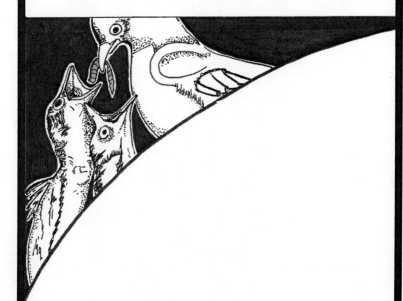

The Art of Mothering

8

*"Life is the first gift, love is the second,
and understanding is the third."*
Marge Piercy

—∞∞∞—

8

WISDOM

The Art of Mothering

My mother told me, "Babies don't come with a roadmap; you have to plot your own course." I needed the wisdom of my mother and other mothers to help me plot my course for it was from their shared wisdom that I first learned to be a mother. This "mother wisdom," passed down from mother to daughter, is not always relayed verbally, but often by example.

As a child, I had models for "mother wisdom" that were numerous and varied. Besides my mother, there were eleven maternal aunts and on my father's side five more, who nearly all lived nearby. We had a custom of visiting each other often. As a young mother, still living in this community, I had a wealth of experience to draw from. I could sort out the good from the bad and develop my own skills.

Now having been a mother for 55 years, a grandmother for 26 years, and a great-grandmother for 8 years, I also realize that this art of mothering requires a special wisdom because each child is unique and has different needs. This wisdom is a compilation of many different elements: practical knowledge, experience, common sense, good judgment, understanding, and compassion. These are all pieces that make up the whole. We need to combine all the pieces in the right proportion to suit the individual child.   This is a real challenge because there is no recipe to follow.

My own experiences as a mother taught me the meaning of a phrase my mother often used "Don't sweat the small stuff!" I had to pick my battles and the bigger issues had to be about what was really important to me. When mothering my eight children I learned by experience that while each child was unique, there were some parenting guidelines that were helpful with all of them:

- Listen to your child and be interested in what he or she has to say; make opportunities for conversations. This helped me guide each child's choices about friends, activities and behaviors.
- Be careful with what you say and how you say it. A child doesn't always take things the way we mean them.
- Apologize when you make a mistake.

Thankfully, "mother wisdom" and personal experience helped me find my own way. The same was true
for the other eight mothers who contributed to this
book. And so it will be for you as well.

Patricia Urban

Shared Wisdom

I've always been told that wisdom comes with age. The definition of "wisdom" from the Encarta World English Dictionary would support the adage, for it says wisdom is "accumulated knowledge of life ... that has been gained through experience."

However, there is another source of wisdom, another source we sometimes forget to tap—other people who have their experiences to share!

When our oldest daughter, Sarah, was pregnant for the first time, she took the responsibility of becoming a mother very seriously. She decided to write letters to mothers whom she knew, including her two grandmothers, her aunts and me. Sarah asked for any words of wisdom they wished to share.

Sarah received many responses, some funny, some philosophical, some very practical. The overwhelming message was to find other mothers or at least one, to walk with on this motherhood journey. Many mothers have discovered the comfort involved in consulting another mother—new, as well as experienced, mothers. Women who have or are experiencing the joys and challenges of motherhood can offer each other advice, support, and sometimes, even that touch of wisdom.

Patricia Bertucci

"If you want to go quickly, go alone. If you want to go far, go together."

—African Proverb

What I learned...

From my mother:
- Never put the baby to bed with a bottle.
- A six month old who can sit in a high chair can drink from a cup.
- Use of a playpen/ pack'n play is practical and safe.
- Bath time can be soothing for everybody and a great way to end a busy day.
- A clean baby is a happy baby.
- You can't hold a baby too much.
- Dads are very capable and love to help from the very beginning.
- You can't introduce books or prayers too soon.
- Rosary beads and a safe perch on the basement stairs make a thunder storm almost bearable.

From my friends:
- The use of irony or sarcasm is lost on the young. Stick to simple, straightforward, and honest.
- If you know a better way to accomplish something, it's your responsibility as a parent to do it for your child.
- Don't underestimate the potential of your child.
- Don't clutter children's bedrooms with electronic equipment like a TV, computer, or video games; leave them in the common areas of the home and allow the bedrooms to be places where dreams can come alive.

From my children:
- Compare siblings at your own risk.
- Listen and don't judge before the offender has had a chance to explain.
- You can pack a lunch but you can't make them eat it.
- Books come in many shapes and sizes and it just takes the right one to make a reader out of a reluctant child.
- Be careful what you say because someone will always remember.
- The best place for conversation can be the car, especially one on one.
- If you start a tradition, i.e. giving a certain gift for high school graduation, you better darn well do it every time even when the graduations are 9 years apart.
- When you're a younger sibling you can learn from the mistakes of the older ones; you don't have to make the mistakes yourself.

By myself:
- Playing outdoors even when it takes a ½ hour to dress for a 15 minute outing is worth every second.
- Birthday parties don't have to be elaborate to be fun. Our main activity used to be decorating your own cupcake and it was a hit every time.
- Best friends aren't what they're cracked up to be. They can move away or put pressure on you or your child to conform to some standard your

family might not be comfortable with. Better to play with and connect with many different friends.

- Any time spent with your children is time well spent.

Jo Ann Figueiredo

The Journey of Mothering

It is always a delight to hear from my youngest sister, Nancy. She has a sunny personality and meets life with a sense of humor. She lives with her husband and two young daughters in France, so we don't get to talk very often.

One day recently she phoned with excitement in her voice. She had just returned from taking Lexi, her 6 year old daughter, to school for the first day of grade one. However, her feelings of happiness were clouded by another concern:

"Lexi and I had a major falling out yesterday. She was awful all morning: running, screaming, sticking out her tongue, defiant and on and on. Finally, I just told her, 'You are not having any ice cream for lunch!' Soon after, Lexi's cousin and her parents arrived for a surprise visit. And, of course, they brought ice cream! I still said, 'NO'. She whimpered into my shoulder for a solid 15 minutes—that was the hardest, not to mention the disapproving looks I got from the rest of the family. But the worst of it—by this time neither Lexi nor I could remember what she had done to warrant the consequence!"

My sister, who is a successful business woman and wonderful mother, was unusually rattled. She worried that she had been too strict and fretted about Lexi's over-all emotional health. She could see the possible causes for her daughter's behavior—fatigue, anxiety over the first day in a new school—and blamed herself for not recognizing it sooner. But none of this made it any easier. Even my words of empathy didn't calm the waters. Oh, how familiar this all felt.

For me, this episode between mother and child seems so normal in its essential ingredients. It exemplifies the journey of mothering. We often find ourselves asking, "Who is this little person? What does she need? What can I do to teach or help her? Why don't I have control? And as her mother, how can I help her navigate this life event?"

We'll be required to answer this last question over and over as our child grows. I hesitate to tell Nancy now, but she can expect the same craziness before Lexi starts middle school, high school, and the whole summer before college. Sometimes, all a mother can do is put a stake in the ground, gathering all one's maternal authority and say, "No ice cream!"—which is to say, "This must stop!" It may be a completely irrelevant consequence but it sets a clear boundary, giving the child a sense of safety and order.

As mothers, we have such a deep desire to do the best for our child—and agonize when we seem to have failed. Thankfully, mothering is a learned skill. We are always learning, from day one until forever. The precious gift is that we get better. We learn more and more about this unique person we are raising and we learn important things about ourselves. We journey together. The building blocks are time and relationship. In the end, it is the consistent loving care that we give our child over the long haul that makes the difference.

Suzanne Shady

"The giving of love is an education in itself."
—Eleanor Roosevelt

Seize the Moment

"How can you be a family if you don't spend time together?" This was a question Father James asked many families who participated in retreats through the years at a monastery in Western New York. A simple answer to this question for our family was "Dinner Time."

When our four daughters were young and involved in activities, eating dinner as a family was a challenge. For the most part, by being flexible, we probably ate together about 95% of the time.

There was a period when my husband, Bob, worked at night. He was present when the girls got home at around 3:30 PM and he left for work at 4:00 PM. During those days we instituted "tea time." When the bus dropped off the girls in the afternoon, we ate dinner together. Then around the usual dinnertime we had a snack, and Bob ate a snack when he returned home at around 11:00 PM. There was the usual complaint that "It's too early for dinner!" The complaining turned into sighs of understanding when they heard, "Yes, but Dad will be with us."

Sports and other outside activities made our dinner times very complicated. Usually, but not always, we could sit together for a little while before or after the activity. If the meal was too close to the time of physical exertion, our daughter ate earlier but sat down with us, so we could be together around the table for a short time at least.

At the beginning of each school year came the deluge of new and wonderful activities that were possible. Each year we would sort out what would fit into our schedule. Given the volume and quality of possibilities, it was difficult to choose. Young children want to do everything without seeing the ramifications of how these choices affect the family. Checking a box and signing on the commitment line can alter the entire family's life. So, we deliberated carefully and limited each child to no more than two major commitments. That would permit time for eating dinner together. If it did not fit we crossed it off the list.

Each moment together is a precious gift that can never be replaced or relived. To seize each moment, being present to one another, will never be regretted.

Patricia Costigan

"It will be gone before you know it. The fingerprints on the wall appear higher and higher then suddenly they are gone."

—Dorothy Enslin

Family Is Family

Our eldest daughter was only four days old when we adopted her. Before she could even walk we told her she was adopted and how very special she was to us. We adopted a puppy when she was four. As she received dolls and stuffed animals, she adopted them. We adopted her brother when she was two. It wasn't until she went to kindergarten that she fully realized that there were other ways to come into a family.

The summer of her twelfth year she became a mother's helper for a family of four little girls. One day the children were playing in the yard. The oldest girl got into an argument with one of her sisters. In a rage she said to her sister, "If you don't stop it I'll tell Mom to put you out for adoption." Overhearing the conversation my daughter said to her, "Sarah, adoption doesn't mean being put out of a family. It means coming into one." When she recounted this conversation to me later that day I smiled knowing that she understood the true meaning of adoption. Family is family no matter how it is formed.

Diane Knittle

All children need a laptop. Not a computer,
but a human laptop.
Moms, Dads, Grannies and Grandpas, Aunts,
Uncles—someone to hold them,
read to them, teach them. Loved ones who will
embrace them and pass on the experience,
rituals and knowledge of a hundred previous
generations. Loved ones who will pass to the
next generation their expectations of them, their
hopes, and their dreams.

—Colin Powell

No Easy Fix

Cape Cod has been a favorite vacation place for my family since I was little. My parents, Aunt Rosemary, three brothers, one sister and I went year after year for two weeks, always staying in Bass River. When my siblings and I had children, we started taking them to the Cape. We were fortunate enough to be able to rent cottages on a small, little-traveled street.

Our daughter Sarah, who is the oldest of all the cousins, remembers when she made a sand castle with Uncle Bob. He was the best at castles with huge structures and neat decorations made of rocks and shells. In the middle of one night after making a particularly special castle, Sarah woke up crying. She did not want the castle washed away when the tide came in. She remembers that night even now twenty-five years later! I could not make the promise that the castle would be there the next day. However I could hug her and just listen. Sarah recently shared that she learned that night that not everything in life can be fixed. She was very glad I could hug her and comfort her, even though I could not save the castle.

Patricia Bertucci

Right under Our Noses

My husband and I were at a pot-luck holiday party when one couple arrived and announced they had brought the Jell-O shots. I had no idea what this was and my curiosity led me to the dining room where the couple had placed a tray filled with shot-glass sized plastic cups containing gelatin infused with vodka.

Something in my memory began to stir. I had seen little plastic cups filled with Jell-O before. In fact, my daughter had prepared them when she was a high-school senior to take as the dessert to a friend's house.

I thought back to that time a few years past when my daughter and her friends were making plans for their Senior Ball. With prom dresses and accessories purchased and dates invited, their attention turned to a pre-dance dinner. One family had offered to host the six couples at their home and the other parents wanted to contribute a dish to the dinner. My daughter opted to bring dessert.

There were a couple of favorite recipes I discussed as possibilities when my daughter said she would make Jell-O. This hardly seemed like a proper dessert but my daughter assured me the girls had decided on it. So I accepted her decision. She would buy the flavor she wanted and prepare it, a simple task.

The day before the dance, I arrived home and was surprised to see the dessert prepared in small plastic cups, not in a mold as I had suggested. I was disappointed in how it looked and said so.

The next day, the day of the dance, my husband thought he would help and bought strawberries and whipped cream to garnish the Jell-O. He halved the strawberries and over our daughter's mild protestations, placed them on top of the Jell-O. It was the best we could do.

We transported daughter, date, and dessert to her friend's home and joined the other parents there in taking pictures and serving dinner to the twelve young guests.

The excitement increased when the limousine arrived to take them to the dance. As they hurried toward the vehicle, I realized that they had not had their dessert. I thought my daughter might feel hurt that her contribution was overlooked, so I opened the refrigerator, grabbed the cookie sheet with the little plastic cups sitting on it and started toward the limo so they could take it with them.

The astute hostess stopped me and quietly said that it would be best not to send the Jell-O, which might spill and ruin the girls' beautiful dresses. She placed it back in her refrigerator.

For a few years I was unaware that our dessert for that event was anything more than what it appeared to be. After learning about Jell-O shots I asked my daughter if there was more to her batch than boiling water and she admitted there was.

Thanks to the wisdom of the other mother, an unwarranted and perhaps disastrous situation was avoided.

I thought my husband and I were pretty aware about where our children were and what they were doing.

This experience made us wiser parents and heightened our vigilance with our younger children.

Sheila Roney

"Mistakes are the usual bridge between inexperience and wisdom."

—Phyllis Theroux

Too Many Tables

Tables not only serve as places to eat but places for children to do homework, for Mom to fold laundry, for Dad to balance the checkbook, for Grandma to make her famous pies, a place to throw the mail and keys, to comfort a disconsolate child, for guests at numerous parties, and more.

Our family of seven has spent a lot of time around the tables in our home. Somehow our family acquired four tables over the course of 41 years. There was the maple kitchen table, the dining room table (given to a son and his wife when they bought their first home), a farm table (with a "keeper drawer" for the Bible and pencils) in the kitchen at the lake house, and Grandma and Grandpa's antique oak table that sat near the window facing the lake for leisurely breakfasts and lunches while watching the activity on the lake. It also served as the overflow table when we became too many at the dining room table, as weddings and friends increased our number.

When the children were small, the maple table was in the eat-in kitchen and was the center of our family life. It bore the mark of a Boy Scout project that Michael drilled into it and the patina of many meals. Eventually, after all the children had moved into adulthood we decided to donate it to charity. Paul, 22, and our youngest of five, was told the table would go when we downsized our lives to a town home. His reaction was one of horror! "But Mom, you can't get rid of THAT table! We had our winter picnic lunches under it and watched Nickelodeon from there! We made our tents and played camping under it! We had our friends over for lunch on it! The girls made their doll tea parties on it!" Sadly, we had to. It would not fit in the new home.

Part of growing up is letting go, so for our son, Paul, letting go of the table meant holding on to the memories dear but letting the table serve another family, unknown to us, to share their lives and build their own memories.

Diane Knittle

Wisdom Gems

Over my 26 years of parenting some things I have learned:

Look At Her Nose

When one of my daughters is expressing her feelings in a most "animated" or difficult manner and she needs to get out her emotions, I detach my ego and look at her nose. In that way she can say what is bothering her and usually talk herself around to the conclusion I would have given to her. I try not to react to her emotions with emotion. Because I am looking at her, she reads it as listening and I do not get caught up in responding with emotion which could jeopardize our relationship.

Bless Her Change Me

When I am having difficulty with a daughter's behavior, I say the little prayer: "Bless her, change me." In that manner grace flows her way to help her in her difficulty. Grace flows my way too, so I can better understand and not judge her.

No Is the Most Important Word in the English Language

My father-in-law gave us these words and we have passed them on to our girls in a sort of mantra. It is healthy to say no in a balanced way to ourselves, i.e., what do we really *need?* It is important to say no to others who ask unreasonable or unhealthy things of us.

Listen, Love and Learn

Each day as our children left to catch the bus for school, my husband said to them, "Listen, love, and learn." They could take this to any relationship or situation they found themselves in during the school day. Today, in their twenties we still hear them say these words.

Patricia Costigan

Better Housekeeping

At the dinner table one evening, my 17-year-old daughter, Caitlyn, confessed she'd been reading my *Good Housekeeping* magazine and that one of the articles had surprised her. She thought the author had meant well, but her methods for raising children were crazy and very different from mine. The author had written that the problem with parents today was that they wanted to be friends with their children and this was turning children into brats.

I knew this shocked her because we share a close bond and I consider my daughter, along with my other children, among my closest friends. As she continued to discuss the points the article made, she shared that the author believed that when children proclaim, "I hate you!" it's a signal that you are raising them properly. I can count on one hand the number of times that all four of my children have said, "I hate you!" By this author's standards, I'd raised my children completely wrong.

After the conversation with Caitlyn, I was driven to read the article myself. I discovered that the author felt very strongly that parents cannot be friends with their children and must demand respect above all else. She shared that it was improper to praise your children, that acknowledging their beauty and brilliance would only end up hurting them later by giving them false ideas. She said that telling your child they are beautiful is a lie that will only set them up for disappointment. She shared that periodically embarrassing children was an appropriate form of punishment, along with adding additional chores to their household duties.

I do not agree. Praise is essential for a child to blossom. You're not lying—you are providing your child with positive reinforcement that will propel them forward and help sustain them throughout their life. Every mother thinks that her child is beautiful, by traditional standards or not, and she should share her feelings with her child. If a mother does not see her child as beautiful, perhaps she should reassess her own values and standards. Also, I think that any sort of punishment must fit the crime of the child, as well as being age appropriate. Children should never be embarrassed or made to feel badly; this can harm them above anything else. Children should respect their parents—this is easy to see—but parents should also respect their children.

Raising children is not a marathon—it's the day-by-day actions and examples that you set for your children. No matter the age of your children, it is your daily role to provide the wisdom bestowed upon you to them. Hopefully, your children will come to see the wisdom within you and seek out your opinion as valuable when they grow older.

Elizabeth O'Toole

Don't Panic, It's All Organic

Every twig woven into our family's nest might represent a decision that my husband and I made through the years. In 2010, the youngest of our six children graduated from university and that was nine years after the graduation of our first child. Now, as my husband and I perch atop our sturdy structure, some twigs jut out and pinch me as I struggle to become comfortable on my empty nest.

One decision in particular still makes me squirm whenever I think about it. Our oldest daughter had returned home after university. We had two others in college at the time, plus three still at home. Her homecoming was joyous and her presence was a welcome addition to our busy home.

Trying to think ahead and wondering what the natural path was for this and other adult children who might be returning after the completion of school, I came up with a plan. I announced—against my husband's wishes but firm in my conviction that this was a great idea—that she could stay 6 months and then she would have to start to pay room and board. We did not need the money, but I thought it would teach some responsibility and maybe encourage her to fly off to her new life on her own. I also assumed that this plan would be inviolable and would work seamlessly if all the graduates returned. Unfortunately the announcement was not received very well and created an artificial stress on the whole household.

She did indeed find a great job back in the city where she had gone to school and was gone for good in short order. My husband saved the rent money and returned it to her years later when she got married.

I could never again enforce this 'would be' grand plan. As the graduates flocked back home, they all seemed to come with a plan. One went to Atlanta with AmeriCorps; the next went to South America for six weeks to immerse himself in the language and culture and then immediately went on to get a master's degree. The fourth child was home briefly but soon enough moved out of town with her job. The fifth one came home, said he'd spend the summer with us and then he was moving to New York City to seek his fortune and he did exactly that. All of a sudden I was left wondering what the hurry had been and feeling somewhat sheepish about the idea that anyone had ever really needed my help to leave home.

I thought I could neatly treat them all the same but found that one size did not fit all. The harshest treatment was meted out to the oldest and that still rankles. If I had to do it over again, I would try harder to see her as an individual and not be so worried about creating an all-encompassing plan. My husband maintained from the beginning that each graduate's choices should be judged on their own merit. After my false start, that is just what we did.

Jo Ann Figueiredo

Twig Wisdom

When my twin sister and I were three, our mother contracted tuberculosis, so we were sent to live with our paternal grandparents. It was a frightening and sad time for both of us. Thankfully, Mom recovered and we were reunited three years later.

Becoming a family again took time. One day I remember my mother complaining to her mother, in exasperation over my sister's behavior, as she had grown into a headstrong and stubborn little girl. My grandmother told her, "You can bend her but do not break her. God gave her personality traits that she will need in her life."

How true this proved to be! My twin grew up, married and had eight children, lost her husband to cancer in middle age, and faced many adversities. She met all of these challenges with strength and tenacity. My mother passed this helpful advice on to me when our little strong-willed child started flexing a stubborn, headstrong muscle. How thankful I am to have had my Gram's advice.

Diane Knittle

"As the twig is bent so grows the tree."

—Proverb

Let Go... and Let God

As a mother of eight, I had to have faith when my husband died from cancer. Two of my children were grown and living on their own, three were in college, two were in high school, and the youngest was in fourth grade.

Suzanne could have gone to college for free until she was 21, as Social Security would have helped. But Sue said she did not want to go to college "like all my siblings." Instead she got a job at a nearby marina. The day after she turned eighteen she came downstairs with her suitcase and said she was going to live at the marina! When my mother-in-law heard this, she invited Sue to come live with her in California. So Sue moved out West and got a job at a drive-in restaurant.

Several months later, my mother-in-law called to tell me that Suzanne had moved out and left a note saying, "Don't worry about me. I'll be fine!" I was ready to catch the next plane to move out there and find her. But how do you find a teenager who does not want to be found in southern California? Besides, I still had two children at home and a job. So we prayed!

Suzanne called me on my birthday. She gave me a phone number where I could reach her. She was living with a man who was twenty years older. We talked every few weeks. I did not have her address nor did my mother-in-law. The following summer I flew out to California to visit. Sue did not let me come to see where she lived, but arranged for us to meet on the beach.

I was wading in the ocean when Sue arrived. We ran to meet each other and hugged in the water, which was a good thing because that way our tears didn't show. I never met her "friend." Shortly after my visit, she moved into an apartment with a girlfriend. She soon realized that the job she had was not very challenging, nor did it pay well. She began to take classes at a community college. She finally earned a bachelor's degree and called me to say, "I got a BS just like all my siblings!" My comment to her was, "Do you think it is in the genes?" Her answer was, "I'm not wearing jeans anymore!"

Suzanne has a great sense of humor. She's also generous with her time. She became a volunteer with the local police station and helped teach at-risk teens to make good choices. She helped plant trees with them and became their role model.

In my experience as a mother I often had to rely on faith and trust. Through that I learned the wisdom to know when to "let go… and let God."

Patricia Urban

"Children are likely to live up to what you believe of them."

—Lady Bird Johnson

Heartfelt Memories

Two publications that I recently read contained the same scripture passage, "Mary kept all these things pondering them in her heart" (Luke 2:19). This led me to think about the heart and some of the emotions we mothers hold there: love, joy, sorrow, worry, courage, fear, frustration. These emotions play different roles at different times, but collectively are the basis for mothering—the art comes from the heart. From infancy to adulthood, we hold our children in our hearts and care for them to the best of our abilities.

Motherhood is an ever-evolving state of life. Because each child is different and continually grows and changes, so must we in order to provide the appropriate guidance and support. What I have learned from conversations with my grown children is that they have an overall impression of childhood happiness or disappointment. They don't always remember the specific details from their childhood events, but they certainly still live in my heart.

One of my children has a memory of not liking a certain teacher but I remember it was because that teacher chose teams by alphabetical order and frequently started at the beginning of the alphabet. Our last name is toward the end so many times my child wasn't chosen. I had to help this child understand that even though it seemed unfair, it probably was not intentional.

Another remembers enjoying nursery school, but I remember being upset because I forgot to send the Valentine cards for the exchange and so my child had to make new ones with supplies at school. As it turned out, she was very happy to do this, and I began to learn that it was okay if I wasn't perfect. And one child remembers the excitement of finally being ready to spend the night at a friend's but I remember holding her hand as we walked to the friend's house and the tears that fell as I walked home by myself, knowing my baby was on the path to independence.

As mothers we are memory makers and keepers and while we want everything to be perfect for our children, it doesn't have to be. And we don't have to be, either. What is important is the love and attention we give. That's what remains and sustains them.

Sheila Roney

Finding Mother Wisdom

"Don't worry, Sue, it's just a stage she's in."

No other words sounded so sweet or brought such relief to my weary, new mother-of-a-toddler ears. I can no longer recall my daughter's exasperating behavior, but I was sure I had failed as a mother, spoiled my child, and would soon go crazy having to deal with it. These words from a more experienced mom gave me hope and renewed my faith in my ability. If this behavior was truly going to end, then I could endure. This "mother wisdom" was shared in a mother's group almost thirty years ago.

My first experience with a mother's group was in Canada in the 1970s, when I was a young married woman without children. Most of my good friends were well into establishing their own families. They met every few weeks in a small apartment with their toddlers and babies when the older children were in school. I remember joining them once or twice and being part of this happy, rambunctious group. There was tea, homemade snacks, heartfelt conversation, and mutual encouragement. Childhood issues and sagas were shared and suggestions offered. There was a feeling of warmth and welcome that nurtured children and adults alike.

Years later, I found myself in Rochester, New York, with a new baby, a new community, and a new role. I knew how important it was to be a mother since I had endured a long seven-year wait for a baby. So, despite having told myself that I would never stop working, I chose to stay at home with my child—I didn't want to miss a thing. I threw myself into the task wholeheartedly.

But what a shock! I was lonely, isolated, missing adult company and struggling with my identity. My days seemed lost in a revolving cycle of cooking, feeding, holding, changing, washing, and nurturing this little being. I was used to satisfying days in the workplace, accomplishing goals and seeing results. In desperation I invited the moms with children I was acquainted with to my home—friends from college, from church, from a recent Italian class, anyone I could think of. To my delight, they all said yes! I learned that most moms welcome an invitation when it includes their children.

Over the years our family moved several times to new communities. In Reston, Virginia, I found myself in the same state of isolation and dearly missed my mother's group. I put a notice in the church bulletin. One mom called me immediately, so we set the next meeting date and soon twelve moms and their children crowded my small living room. Reston was filled with young families who were transplants from elsewhere and were anxious to meet new people. Very soon we had twenty-plus moms who had ideas for activities, speakers, and retreat days. How sad I was to have to move again after just eighteen months with these delightful women.

So, filled with enthusiasm, I did the same thing soon after we arrived in Lawrenceville, New Jersey. I placed an ad in the church bulletin—not one response! This time I learned that every community is different. The social ties were already tightly knit in this well-established community.

Thankfully, my children were now school age and I discovered that was a great way to meet other moms and families. In this environment, "mother wisdom" was found as we chatted in the parking lot waiting to pick up children from school, at school fund-raising events, or on the sidelines of the sports field. Moms everywhere talk about their children and compare notes. I was learning from others whose technique and style I appreciated. I emulated a friend's calm, peaceful manner with her children and the clear, direct manner of speech she used to guide them through routines and events. I listened to a beloved European teacher exclaim that Americans ask their children too many questions: "Children can trust their parents to provide a healthy lunch, without a menu of choices, and should just eat it!" I tried out different parenting skills and learned what worked for my family.

The need for "mother wisdom" never ends. We moved back to Rochester and as the children began to leave the nest, there was a strong impetus among those early mother's group friends to re-connect after thirty years. We meet at a restaurant over dinner and a glass of wine two or three times a year.

And little did I realize that when we nine women got together to write a book, we'd become a mother's group for one another. Our meetings always start with a simple pot-luck supper. There is non-stop conversation, much laughter, and sometimes tears. We take great comfort in the insights and suggestions exchanged as we face the challenges and complexities of parenting our adult children, nurturing aging parents and understanding the empty nest stage of our lives.

How much I owe to my mother's group friends! They have taught me about unconditional love, the importance of family, and the strength and sustenance of faith on life's journey. Most importantly, I have learned the collective wisdom that is to be found in a circle of moms.

Suzanne Shady

Our Thanks

*It takes a village...................*to help nine ordinary moms write a book! This project, that grew larger and took longer than we ever dreamed, was completed with the generous assistance of many people who deserve our special thanks.

Our husbands and children encouraged us and provided hours of assistance through patient listening, chatting to refresh memories and hands-on help in a variety of ways. They graciously allowed us to reveal the details of their personal lives and they motivated us to persevere.

Our mothers, sisters and extended family were a source of rich ideas and continued support.

Mary Jane Ryan, our developmental editor and noted author, understood our vision and brought our manuscript to maturity through her insightful and judicious editing skills. Her expertise, which bordered on the miraculous to us, gave us a finished product to be proud of and enabled us to make our dream a reality.

Tracy Schuhmacher critiqued and edited our early efforts and taught us the basics of good story writing. Joan Mondello shared her invaluable expertise in project management and helped us develop our mission and vision statements, and a process for coordinating nine collaborative authors. Mary Jo Brach read our finished manuscript and her thorough review inspired us to revise our text in many important ways. Their enthusiasm and encouragement gave us confidence that we could achieve our goal.

Suzanne Johnston, Sister Kay Lurz, SSJ, Ruth Lawrence, MD and Rev. Robert Madden, CSB offered helpful suggestions and advice after reading our manuscript. Sara McLaughlin and Ray Shady did a careful editing of the finished first draft.

Many Educators, Pastors, Pastoral Staff and parents participated in our Focus Group Survey. Not only did they contribute to a deeper understanding of the needs and stresses facing parents today, but they also helped us stay on track and true to the goals of our book.

Cheryl Bennett and James Montanus provided our cover photo and assisted with several technical design requirements.

Fr. Tony Mugavero contributed his practical insight, gentle counsel and prayers. Brother James and the monks at Mt. Savior Monastery offered their wisdom and hospitality during our "writing retreat."

~~~~~

Our goal was to write a book; our gift was that we found each other. The authors, some friends and some acquaintances, came together for the first time on December 12, the feast day of Our Lady of Guadalupe, the pregnant Madonna. All nine of us experienced her guidance, influence and grace as we were writing *Mothering, an Art of the Heart.* For this we are very grateful.

About the Authors

Patricia Bertucci graduated from college with a BA in English and taught for four years at a Catholic elementary school. Then she embarked on her journey as a stay-at-home mom for 19 years. During that time she was very involved with her four children's schools, her parish, mothers' groups and community service such as Refugee Family Resettlement. Next she returned to teaching and earned her MS in Elementary Education. After 17 years in the classroom, she still enjoys teaching fourth graders and treasures time with her husband, Jon, her four children and two grandchildren.

Patricia Costigan and her husband, Bob, have four beautiful daughters, Clare, Beth, Anne and Irene. Before children, she earned a BA in Art and an MA in Special Education, taught and always made art. Through the years she has been involved with local and international social justice issues. Pat recently completed a series of paintings on "Hope" and is working on a new series titled "Grace." Pat designed and created the artwork and illustrations for this book. When she is not busy in her studio, she is often found walking her rescue dog, Bella, around her neighborhood in Fairport, NY.

Jo Ann Figueiredo and her husband, Rui, are the parents of six children, Sara, Kate, Joe, Emily, Steve and Mari and they are grandparents to five grandchildren under the age of three. She is a graduate of the University of St. Michael's College at the University of Toronto where she earned a B.A. in English Literature. She worked as a paralegal for a Toronto law firm and as a nursery school teacher, then left to focus her time and talent for 22 years on raising a family. Currently she is in her tenth year as a Teacher's Assistant for two second grade classes at Seton Catholic School. Jo Ann has volunteered extensively in her children's schools and in her parish serving as a High School Board Member, Chairperson of the Sports Association, Religious Education teacher and Marriage Preparation leader. Presently, she serves on her parish Pastoral Council and is actively working for her high school alma mater in fund raising. Jo Ann lives with Rui in her hometown of Rochester, NY and loves the printed word almost as much as she loves her family.

Diane Knittle has a BA from Dominican University and taught primary grades until she and Bill adopted their first child. She was a volunteer in both the children's school and for the Diocese of Rochester during her 24 years as a stay-at-home mom. She obtained a Master's Degree in Theology and Pastoral Counseling and training in Clinical Pastoral Education in 1991. She enjoyed the next 20 years as a Parish Pastoral Associate, a hospital chaplain and a Catholic chaplain in a long term care facility. In retirement, she is a hospice volunteer and tutors at Nativity School, Rochester NY. She and her husband, Bill, have five married children and four grandchildren.

Mary Dahl Maher's life ambition to become a medical missionary in South America was side-tracked when she met and married another student in her global undergraduate program. She and Ken have shared 40 years of adventures from East Africa to Mexico, but have been settled in Rochester, New York for the last 23 years. They are parents to seven children and grandparents to nine. Mary intermittently home-schooled each of her children and was involved in church and community activities such as teaching childbirth education classes and Children's Creative Response to Conflict courses. Her belief that peace begins in the womb and her commitment to the power of motherhood led to a second career as a Certified Nurse-Midwife. She currently shares that passion as a nursing professor and is completing doctoral research on the birth outcomes of Latina migrant farm worker women.

Elizabeth O'Toole's passion is children, whether at home, in the schools, in church, or in the library. Prior to marriage she was an Elementary Education/Special Education teacher. Later, as a Navy wife, Liz was an at-home mom for 18 years with her four children, now ages 19-26. When her youngest entered school, she became an evening clerk in the local library. Her job evolved into a full-time position as a Youth Services Public Librarian, which she has held for the last 14 years. She has volunteered extensively in youth ministry, church, and schools. Liz lives in Walworth, NY with her husband, John, and dog, Miss Daisy.

Sheila Roney has three children, Bridget, Brian and Caitlin. Upon completing her BA, she taught in a Catholic elementary school, and then left that position to be a stay-at-home mom when her oldest was born. While raising her children she held volunteer positions in her parish and her children's schools. For several years she worked part-time as a Teacher Assistant providing extra literacy support to individual students. Eventually, she earned an MS in Education and worked with emergent and struggling readers as a reading specialist in a public school for 11 years. She and her husband, Bob, are currently enjoying retirement in their homes in New York and Florida.

Suzanne Shady is the mother of two children, Anna Mary and Raymond III, who were her "miracle babies" and the answer to her heart's desire. She is a Certified Catholic Chaplain working in hospital, brain injury rehabilitation and mental health care settings. After college she worked for eight years with emotionally disturbed and/or physically disabled children, was an early childhood research assistant and community organizer. When her children arrived Sue devoted herself to family as a stay- at- home mom for 20 years. She initiated mother's groups in several communities when the family relocated and became an active volunteer in school and parish. She has a BA in Psychology, training in Clinical Pastoral Education and earned an MA in Theology from St. Bernard's School of Theology and Ministry. She and her husband, Ray, are blessed with two grandchildren and live outside Rochester, NY.

Patricia Urban is the mother of eight children ages 44 to 56 (two deceased). She was widowed when her husband, Richard, died at the age of 45 and her youngest child was ten. In order to support her family she returned to school, earned a BS in Education and taught in Catholic elementary schools for 20 years. After retiring, Pat became a Claretion Volunteer, serving for two years in a disadvantaged, inner city parish in New Jersey. She has been an active volunteer in her church, working with youth groups on social justice projects and in prison ministry, conducting retreats for incarcerated men and women. She enjoys traveling, especially to visit her six loving children, thirteen grandchildren and one great grandchild.

BUILDING A STRONG FAMILY

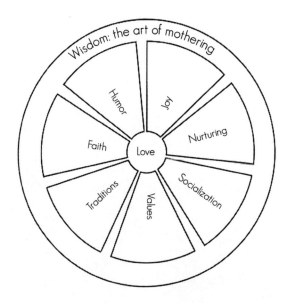

THE WHEEL ICON

The icon of the wheel is a visual representation of the elements that help build a strong family. The eight elements we have identified are Love, Joy, Nurturing, Socialization, Values, Traditions, Faith and Humor. The balance of these elements establishes the integrity of the whole.

Love is at the center, providing the framework to strengthen and unify the elements. Wisdom, the art of mothering, is the outer rim that encircles the family to maintain harmony and stability.

CPSIA information can be obtained at www.ICGtesting.com
Printed in the USA
BVOW08s2206240913

332063BV00001B/18/P